Product

MW00677788

THE

Microsoft®

PUBLISHED BY
Microsoft Press
A Division of Microsoft Corporation
One Microsoft Way
Redmond, Washington 98052-6399

Library of Congress Cataloging-in-Publication Data
Seroshek, Steve, 1972-
    The Pocket PC / Steve Seroshek.
      p. cm.
    Includes index.
    ISBN 0-7356-1159-9
    1. Pocket computers. I. Title.

QA76.5 .S435 2001
004.16--dc21   00-069441

Printed and bound in the United States of America.

3 4 5 6 7 8 9   MLML   6 5 4 3 2

Distributed in Canada by Penguin Books Canada Limited.

A CIP catalogue record for this book is available from the British Library.

Microsoft Press books are available through booksellers and distributors worldwide.
For further information about international editions, contact your local Microsoft
Corporation office or contact Microsoft Press International directly at fax (425) 936-
7329. Visit our Web site at mspress.microsoft.com. Send comments to
mspinput@microsoft.com.

ActiveSync, ActiveX, Hotmail, Microsoft, the Microsoft Internet Explorer logo,
Microsoft Press, MSN, Outlook, SideWinder, Windows, the Windows logo, Windows
Media, and Windows NT are either registered trademarks or trademarks of Microsoft
Corporation in the United States and/or other countries. Other product and company
names mentioned herein may be the trademarks of their respective owners.

Unless otherwise noted, the example companies, organizations, products, people, and
events depicted herein are fictitious. No association with any real company, organization, product, person, or event is intended or should be inferred.

Acquisitions Editor: Alex Blanton
Project Editor: Rebecca McKay
Technical Editor: Julie Xiao

To my family and friends for their patience during the creation of this book, and especially to my loving wife, Karolyn, for all her support.

Contents

Contents

Contents

Introduction

The Pocket PC is an amazing product! You will not find a more complete, feature-rich personal digital assistant (PDA) on the market. The Pocket PC is essentially a toolbox containing the tools to enable you to become more productive in your everyday tasks. The Pocket PC also gives you the freedom to connect to the Internet, play color-enriched games, listen to digital music, and more. If you are a software developer, you can use standard Windows-based tools to create unlimited custom applications to suit your needs.

I expect the reader of this book to be anybody new to the Pocket PC or anybody looking for a Pocket PC reference. If you are already a Pocket PC expert, this book is probably not for you.

Throughout this book, you will find step-by-step guides and helpful hints for connecting to the Internet, downloading digital music to the Pocket PC, and much more. I've tried to make the processes in this book as simple as possible without including too much unnecessary technical babble.

This book is not designed to be your only resource for the Pocket PC. The Pocket PC is a complex product. In fact, each topic covered in the following chapters could potentially be a book in itself. As with any great product, you can find other helpful resources through books and Web sites. The Pocket PC Web site (*www.PocketPC.com*) is a good place to start.

Corrections, Comments, and Help

Every effort has been made to ensure the accuracy of this book. Microsoft Press provides corrections and additional content for its books through the World Wide Web at:

http://mspress.microsoft.com/support

If you have comments, questions, or ideas regarding this book, please send them to us.

Send e-mail to:

msinput@microsoft.com

Or send postal mail to:

Microsoft Press
Attn: The Pocket PC Editor
One Microsoft Way
Redmond, WA 98052-6399

Please note that support for the Pocket PC itself is not offered through the above addresses.

Visit the Microsoft Press World Wide Web Site

We invite you to visit the Microsoft Press World Wide Web site at the following location:

http://mspress.microsoft.com

You'll find descriptions of our books, information about ordering titles, notices of special features and events, additional content for Microsoft Press books, and much more.

You can also find the latest in software development and news from Microsoft Corporation by visiting the following World Wide Web site:

http://www.microsoft.com

We look forward to your visit on the Web!

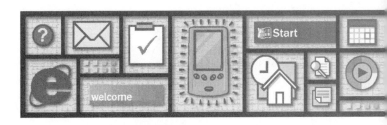

1

The PC in Your Pocket

When personal computers (PCs) began to gain popularity in the late 1980s, they were monster machines with little computing power, especially compared with today's standards. Since the introduction of the PC, however, the personal computing industry has worked to shrink the size and increase the performance of the PC.

When I graduated from high school, I received a laptop as a graduation gift. At the time, it was a top-of-the-line model—a whopping 386SX with 12 MB of RAM! I'm amazed when I think back to that laptop and realize how computing devices have morphed from desktop to laptop to even smaller computers. Today my wristwatch probably has more computing power than that laptop did. (OK, I'm exaggerating—but you understand what I mean.)

Even with the popularity of the laptop, people still searched for a smaller computing device that could handle their needs. The personal digital assistant (PDA) was created to help people access information at any time or any place. A number of companies have released several iterations of the PDA, most of which are limited to personal information management (PIM). PIM software allows you to record your contact information, appointments, and small tasks. However, as people become more mobile, they want their PDAs to have much of the functionality offered by their desktop PCs, such as the ability to send and receive e-mail and to browse the Web. One PDA offers all these functions and a whole lot more: the Pocket PC.

What Is the Pocket PC?

In general, the Pocket PC is a personal computing device that allows you to keep track of your personal information, such as contacts, appointments, and tasks. But the Pocket PC can be used for more than just PIM functions. The Pocket PC also brings you a multimedia experience like no other. You can listen to digital music, play videos, and read electronic books on the Pocket PC. In fact, you can even listen to digital music while you're reading an electronic book or scanning for upcoming appointments in your calendar.

In size and shape, the Pocket PC resembles a large calculator, not unlike the scientific calculator you might have used in college. All the Pocket PCs available today come with an instruction manual and a CD-ROM that contains Microsoft ActiveSync software and other software goodies. Pocket PCs use Microsoft Windows CE as the base operating system, offer a touch screen to enter information, and have external hardware buttons that can be used for fast access to programs on the device. Pocket PCs also offer some method of expandability, such as a CompactFlash slot, and have docking cradles that allow you to connect your Pocket PC to your desktop or laptop PC and synchronize data between the two.

Pocket PC Hardware

Several original equipment manufacturers (OEMs), such as Casio, Compaq, Hewlett-Packard, and Symbol, build Pocket PCs. Although different models of the Pocket PC are available, the basic operations are almost identical. Where the Pocket PC varies between models is in the hardware. Some devices are slimmer than others. Some might have more memory or execute programs faster. The screen technology might also be different.

The various models range in processing speed from 131 MHz to 206 MHz. The memory can range from 16 MB to 32 MB, which allows for a lot of on-device data and application storage. All models have touch screens for basic user input and navigation instead of a mouse and a keyboard. You can use your finger to tap the screen to navigate, or you can use a penlike apparatus called a stylus, which comes with every Pocket PC. With the stylus, you can write on the screen of the Pocket PC in your own handwriting, using electronic ink. You can also use an on-screen keyboard called a soft keyboard to enter information. In addition to using the touch screen, you can navigate between programs with hardware buttons on the exterior of the Pocket PC. The hardware buttons are preprogrammed for different program functions and navigation.

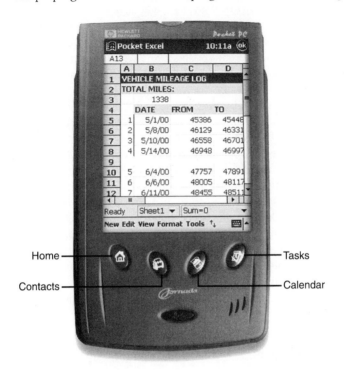

Unlike a desktop or laptop computer, the Pocket PC doesn't contain a hard drive. Instead, all information, including the operating system, is stored in memory. The Pocket PC actually contains a series of circuit chips, together called a *module*, onto which Windows CE has been "burned." What I mean by burned is that the operating system has been downloaded to a read-only-memory (ROM) module at the factory. This is typically a one-time burn, which means the download is permanent. You can't lose portions of the operating system—or the entire operating system itself—as you can on a desktop PC. The likelihood of a corrupt file in ROM is minimal because the operating system is somewhat protected from the rest of the memory on the device. When the operating system is in ROM, you can quickly open and close programs. The device also starts, or boots, quickly.

Upgrading a Pocket PC is a matter of removing the ROM chip and replacing it with an updated version. As simple as this sounds, it might not always be easy because your particular model might not be upgradable. (The OEM that made your Pocket PC will have information on whether you can upgrade your Pocket PC.) The Compaq iPaq model is nice for upgrades because it has a flashable ROM chip that can be reflashed several times with different updates if and when they become available. Flashable ROM is similar to burned ROM in that flashable ROM can be upgraded by the Pocket PC user. You can also flash this kind of ROM several times, whereas burned chips can be modified only once at the factory.

Now that you've learned a little about ROM and how it's used in the Pocket PC, let's talk about random access memory (RAM). RAM is similar to ROM, but RAM allows the operating system to add and remove files, while ROM allows the operating system only to read files. On the Pocket PC, all your personal data is stored in RAM. The programs that you install on your Pocket PC will also be stored in RAM unless you store those programs on a memory storage card. (See Chapter 2 for more information on using memory storage cards with the Pocket PC.)

Feeling confused about ROM and RAM? Just remember that ROM is where the operating system and other programs included with the Pocket PC are stored. RAM is where your data and the programs that *you* install are stored.

Pocket PC Software

Software on the Pocket PC is essentially the same on all models. Windows CE 3.0 is the operating system that controls all the functions on the Pocket PC. You might think that Windows CE is similar to the Windows operating system on your desktop PC. Well, Windows CE is similar in appearance, but it's quite different in architecture and functionality.

Popular applications such as Microsoft Pocket Word, Microsoft Pocket Excel, Microsoft Windows Media Player, and Microsoft Reader are available on all Pocket PC models. Pocket PCs also have ActiveSync, a software program that lets you synchronize data between your Pocket PC and your desktop or laptop PC.

By connecting the Pocket PC to the desktop PC, you can transfer data between the two and update both. For example, if you have a meeting with new clients, you can use the Pocket PC to collect their contact information. When you get back to your office, you can connect the Pocket PC to your desktop PC and transfer the data. Likewise, when you update or add an appointment, a contact, or a task to the desktop PC, the data will be updated on the Pocket PC. This happens automatically when you connect the two devices and either the Pocket PC or the desktop PC detects a change in data.

ActiveSync is also the main software program used when installing programs and viewing content on the Pocket PC. (I'll discuss ActiveSync in greater detail in Chapter 3.)

Out of the Box—Now What?

If you're like me, you probably couldn't wait to get your Pocket PC out of the box and turn it on. In fact, you probably have it all set up and are now listening to digital music. In case you haven't, though, I'll show you how to configure the Pocket PC for first-time use and then tell you how to use the device.

Setting Up the Pocket PC for the First Time

To begin, turn on the Pocket PC. Because the location of the on/off button is different for each model, you might need to refer to the instruction manual for the exact location of this button. The first screen that appears is the Welcome Wizard, which does two things. First, it configures the device for initial use. By following the instructions in the wizard, you'll align the screen and set the time zone for the device. Second, the Welcome Wizard helps familiarize you with some of the basic operations of the Pocket PC, such as tap and hold.

Where's the Right Click?

Unlike your desktop PC, the Pocket PC has no mouse or mouse cursor. Your stylus or fingernail takes the place of the mouse. You tap an item on the screen, such as an icon for a program, to start it or open it.

By clicking the right button on a mouse, you can open a shortcut or context menu in Windows or in a program running in Windows. This ability is called secondary click, or right click. The equivalent of the right click on the Pocket PC is *tap and hold*. Depending on what program you're using, you're presented with a shortcut menu to several quick functions when you tap and hold. For example, when you're in Notes and you want to delete a note, all you have to do is tap and hold the note to open a shortcut menu. Then, on the shortcut menu, tap Delete.

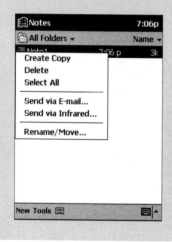

Finding Your Way Around

Some Pocket PC features are similar in look and function to desktop and laptop PCs, while others are different. For instance, you can access just about everything you need on the Pocket PC from the Start menu, such as programs and settings for the device. Unlike the Start menu in desktop Windows, however, the Start menu on the Pocket PC is located in the upper left of the screen.

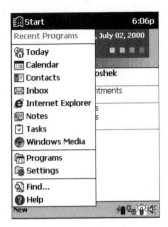

In addition to Programs and Settings on the Start menu, you'll see the programs and features that are installed on every Pocket PC, such as Calendar, Contacts, Internet Explorer, Notes, Tasks, Windows Media, Find, and Help. Many of these programs and features will be familiar to you because they're similar to programs and features on your desktop PC. We'll explore them in more detail in later chapters in this book. Right now, let's look at a few things that are different about the Pocket PC.

Moving Programs on the Start Menu

After you add a program to your Pocket PC, you can usually find it by tapping Start and then tapping Programs. However, you might want to access your most frequently used programs directly from the Start menu so you can get to them faster. To move programs on the Start menu, tap the Start button and then tap Settings. On the Settings screen, tap Menus. On the Menus screen, tap the check boxes next to the items that you want to change on the Start menu. Selecting a check box will add an item to your Start menu; clearing a check box will remove an item from the Start menu.

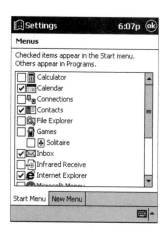

Using the Today Screen

The Today screen, which you can access from the Start menu, allows you to see at a glance what you have planned for the day. You can also open the Calendar to see the agenda for the current day, but the Today screen has your upcoming appointments and tasks all in a single location.

The Today screen is customizable. To add and remove items from the Today screen, tap the Start button and then tap Settings. On the Settings menu, tap Today. From the Today settings screen, you can change the appearance and the order in which the items appear on the Today screen.

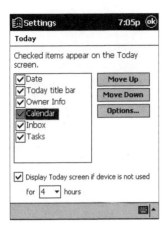

Entering Information

One of the things I like best about the Pocket PC is the ease with which you can enter information. Yes, I enjoy listening to recordings and reading electronic books also, but entering information is so simple that it has become one of my favorite ways to use the Pocket PC.

Soft Keyboard

On the desktop PC, the most common way to enter information is with the keyboard. The same holds true for the Pocket PC except that you use an on-screen, or *soft*, keyboard. The soft keyboard offers the same layout and functionality as a full-size one. To access the soft keyboard, select the keyboard icon in the lower right corner of the screen. If you don't see a keyboard icon, tap the arrow in the lower right corner, and then tap Keyboard on the menu.

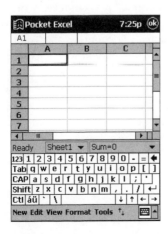

Character Recognizer

Another way to enter information is by writing. With the Character Recognizer on the Pocket PC, you can use handwriting as a method of input. The Pocket PC converts your handwriting to plain text almost as fast as you can write on the screen. Unlike other personal digital assistants (PDAs), the Pocket PC doesn't require that you learn a special alphabet. Granted, your handwriting must be somewhat legible. When I first used this feature, I needed to modify my penmanship a tad for my Pocket PC to accept all of my handwriting. Now I can enter information faster by writing than I can by tapping individual letters on the soft keyboard.

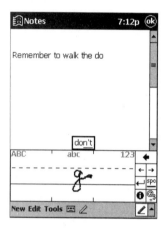

The Transcriber

Another way to enter information is through the Transcriber. The Transcriber is a natural handwriting recognition utility that you can install from the CD-ROM that comes with your Pocket PC. You can find it in the CD-ROM's Extras folder. The Transcriber reliably recognizes words and phrases in cursive, print, and mixed cursive and print styles. By combining the soft keyboard and the Character Recognizer, the Transcriber allows you to make drawing strokes on the screen to backspace and remove characters without having to hit the backspace key on the keyboard. It also provides several options for you to customize the color of the ink, the width of strokes, and so on.

Sound Recording

The final method of entering information is sound recording. Using the Notes program on the Pocket PC, you can record sounds with just a tap on the screen. You can then save that recording and send it to a colleague through e-mail.

Tapping the Record button on the screen is one way to make a recording or a voice note. You can also use the external hardware buttons on the device to make a voice note. The voice-recording button is usually on the upper left side of the exterior of the Pocket PC. By pressing and holding the button, you can make a voice note. When you're done recording, release the button; the voice note is stored in Notes as Recording1, Recording2, and so on. Tap and hold the file to rename it or change the storage location. You can also delete the file by using the same tap-and-hold feature. The purpose of the voice recorder is to record *quick* thoughts, so be warned that the more recordings you make, the more memory is consumed.

After learning about all these ways to enter information, you might expect the Pocket PC to translate speech to text. I hate to disappoint you, but it can't. Give the Pocket PC a few more years, though, and I wouldn't be surprised to see this happen.

Summing Up

The Pocket PC is a powerful device that offers you the basics of personal information management plus a lot more with Microsoft Internet Explorer for the Pocket PC, Pocket Word, Pocket Excel, Pocket Money, Microsoft Reader, and Windows Media Player. The Pocket PC is also expandable and customizable to your needs. As you'll see in the next chapter, the Pocket PC can be expanded to allow you to access the Internet or customized for more specialized purposes such as reading bar codes.

Expand Your Pocket PC

The Pocket PC is a diverse tool that can accomplish a lot of tasks. Right out of the box, the Pocket PC has the ability to do many simple functions, such as personal information management (PIM). But what about browsing the Web and sending and receiving e-mail? Those tasks are a primary reason why we use our desktop PCs. With the Pocket PC, you can do these things—only in a smaller box.

However, if you want to connect to the Internet on the Pocket PC, you need to add a modem. This chapter will show you how to do that and how to expand the Pocket PC with other peripheral devices, such as memory cards, global positioning system (GPS) receivers, and so on. You'll be able to identify the different types of add-ons and understand the technology that allows these components to work with the Pocket PC.

Adding Components to the Pocket PC

The many types of available add-ons for the Pocket PC let you customize your use of the device to match your lifestyle. Do you want to go wireless or use your Pocket PC as a bar code reader? The special expansion slot on the Pocket PC enables you to do either of these things with an expansion card. The possibilities are almost endless.

CompactFlash Technology

The technology behind the expansion capabilities of the Pocket PC is called CompactFlash, or CF. CompactFlash is an industry standard for a peripheral technology used with many consumer electronic devices such as digital cameras and personal digital assistants (PDAs). A CF peripheral device is a small card about the size of a matchbook.

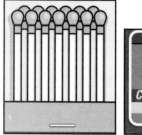

Keep in mind that the CF card isn't a PCMCIA card (PC card). PCMCIA cards are larger and are based on a different standard. The two types of cards, however, have similar uses: they are available as memory cards or as peripheral devices such as modems and network cards.

Most Pocket PCs have a CF card expansion slot built right into the device. The Compaq iPaq is currently the only Pocket PC that gives you an option for either a PCMCIA card or a CF card. You can also use a PCMCIA-to-CF adapter to allow a CF card to work in a PCMCIA slot.

As with PCMCIA cards, there are two types of CF cards—Type I and Type II—which differ in size. Type I is thinner than Type II, and some Pocket PCs and digital cameras offer only a Type I slot. This isn't too inconvenient because most peripheral devices come in the Type I size, which helps reduce the overall thickness of the device. However, some components are available as Type II only. Be sure to identify your type of CF slot and purchase the correct size of card.

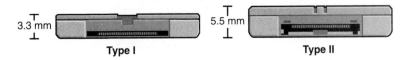

Type I   Type II

Types of CF Cards

CF technology seems simple enough—you purchase an expansion card and insert it into the Pocket PC. What's the catch? Well, there is no catch. Because the Pocket PC uses the CompactFlash industry standard, you don't need to do anything more; insert the card, and you're up and running. On occasion, you might need to install a software driver for the card, but this is rare. Many popular CF cards will work without additional software. That's because the drivers for those cards were built into the operating system of the Pocket PC. When you insert such a card, it's recognized by the system and is ready to use.

Let's take a look at the expandability options available for the Pocket PC.

Memory

In the first chapter, I covered RAM and ROM and how those memory types were built into the Pocket PC. Another type of memory is called CF memory. As we use the Pocket PC for more advanced activities, such as playing videos and music, the need for memory increases accordingly.

CF memory cards come in different sizes, ranging from 8 MB to 340 MB. Most of the newer CF memory cards are Type I. When you're deciding which memory card to purchase, keep in mind that more memory is better, but you don't want to purchase more memory than you think you're going to use. Memory can be expensive.

You can use memory cards for different functions on the Pocket PC. For example, I like to keep separate CF memory cards for digital music, miscellaneous programs, videos, and games. This helps me keep each type of information organized.

Modems

Internet connectivity for Web browsing and e-mail is an essential part of our daily lives. Out of the box, the Pocket PC gives you all the software tools to browse the Web and to send and receive e-mail, but some Pocket

PCs don't have built-in modems. You can't do much online activity without a modem, so that will probably be one of the first items that you purchase if your Pocket PC doesn't have a modem.

Unlike memory cards, only a few types of modems are available for the Pocket PC, and the ones that are available have similar specifications. The common rule when buying a modem is that faster is better. Because most modems have pretty much the same speed, this won't be much of an issue. The recommended, most widely available modems are 56K v.90 modems.

Although a speed of 56 kilobits per second is standard, the physical sizes of the modems aren't. You can purchase both Type I and Type II modems. The type that you need to purchase depends on the type that your Pocket PC supports. If you have a Pocket PC that has a Type I slot, you need to purchase a Type I modem. Conversely, if you have a Pocket PC with a Type II slot, the modem you purchase should be a Type II. Some Pocket PCs, however, can accept Type I and Type II CF cards, giving you a larger selection of CF components that you can buy.

Global Positioning System

Imagine taking your Pocket PC with you on a hiking adventure or mountain bike trip. Several Pocket PC owners have already done this. You can add a GPS to your Pocket PC by utilizing the expandability of the PCMCIA expansion jacket on the Compaq iPAQ or the serial connections of the Casio Cassiopeia and the Hewlett-Packard Jornada 500 series.

A couple of companies provide great GPS solutions for the Pocket PC: Pharos (*http://www.pharosgps.com*) and Teletype (*http://www.teletype. com*). Both solutions offer mapping software and additional hardware components.

Other Expansion Devices

Let's say you want to do other tasks besides connecting with a modem. How about connecting your Pocket PC wirelessly? No problem—all you need is a digital phone card, which uses CF technology to connect a Pocket PC with a cellular phone. (See Chapter 7 for more information about digital phone cards.)

Bluetooth will also play an important role in the way we expand small devices such as the Pocket PC. What is Bluetooth? It's a specification of short-range radio links between wireless phones, mobile and stationary PCs, and peripheral devices. The purpose of Bluetooth is to connect electronic devices without cables. For example, with a Bluetooth-enabled device, you'll be able to connect your Pocket PC to the Internet wirelessly with the mobile phone in your briefcase. The mobile phone will do all of the work without straining the batteries of the Pocket PC. Today you would need to run a cable from your Pocket PC to the mobile phone to connect to the Internet.

Another application of Bluetooth technology might be receiving information about products and special discount savings on your Pocket PC as you walk up and down the aisles of a grocery store.

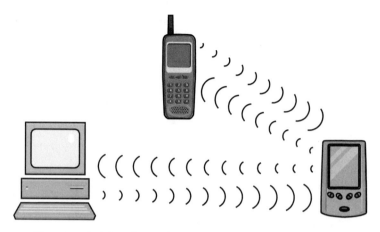

Keep in mind that the Pocket PC isn't just for personal use. It can also be used in business or enterprise environments. With the addition of a bar code scanner, for example, you can turn the Pocket PC into an inventory control device and use it to keep track of items in a custom database.

Summing Up

The Pocket PC can grow with your needs. With the CF expansion slot, you can add other industry-standard components, such as memory cards, modems, GPS cards, bar code readers, and more to your Pocket PC. There is almost no limit to the expandability of the Pocket PC.

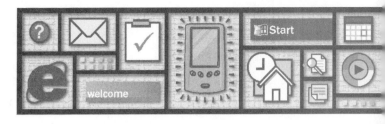

3

Microsoft ActiveSync

The Pocket PC is a great stand-alone device: you can keep track of your contacts and appointments without ever connecting it to the desktop PC. If you never connect the two, though, you'll be missing out on a whole other way to use the Pocket PC. By connecting it to a desktop PC, you can install programs on your device and synchronize information between the two. When you synchronize the information, you ensure that data on the desktop PC is the same as on the Pocket PC. If you change data on the Pocket PC, those changes will be made on the desktop PC when the two machines are synchronized, and vice versa. Microsoft ActiveSync is the program that makes all of this possible.

ActiveSync is the communication bridge between the Pocket PC and the desktop PC. Not only does ActiveSync handle the functions of synchronization, it also moves simple data from the Pocket PC to the desktop PC. For example, suppose you need to move a document from your device to the desktop PC. One way to do it is to synchronize that document. You can also manually move the document using the Windows drag-and-drop method. (I'll cover these methods in more detail later in this chapter.)

In addition to moving data, ActiveSync gives you the ability to install a program on the Pocket PC. You install most programs on the device from the desktop PC using ActiveSync. Before you install ActiveSync, you need to connect your Pocket PC to your desktop PC.

Types of Connections

You have a few different ways to connect a desktop PC with your Pocket PC, including serial, universal serial bus (USB), and infrared connections.

Handheld devices that were available prior to the release of the Pocket PC were usually connected to the desktop PC through a serial connection. Serial cables have nine connection pins on either end and connect to serial ports. Because a serial cable has a data limitation of 115.2 kilobits per second (Kbps), transferring large amounts of information via this type of connection can be tedious.

Most of the new Pocket PCs have USB, which is a faster, more robust interface for transferring information. Because USB connections are less resource-dependent than serial connections, you'll have fewer problems configuring the Pocket PC to connect to the desktop PC through a USB connection. Typically, you just connect the USB cable from the USB port on the Pocket PC to the desktop PC's USB port, and the appropriate software is automatically installed and the connection is established. The only thing that you need to ensure is that the Allow USB Connection With This Desktop Computer check box is selected in the Connection Settings dialog box in ActiveSync.

Infrared is the third method of connectivity. Similar to the way that your television remote control works, infrared data can be beamed between two Pocket PCs or between the desktop PC and the Pocket PC. Easy to use, infrared is a great connection to make between laptops and Pocket PCs because laptops usually have built-in infrared ports.

> **Tip** If you're using a laptop with infrared and you can't get the connection to work, ensure that the infrared, or IR, port is enabled in the CMOS of the laptop. If you're unfamiliar with the CMOS, consult the owner's manual for your laptop for more information.

If you want to use an infrared connection with a desktop PC, you usually have to purchase an external infrared unit that connects to the serial port on the back of the PC. Because all of the Pocket PCs on the market have an infrared port, they're great for cableless connections.

To move data between your Pocket PC and your desktop PC, you'll need to connect an external IR adapter to the serial port and make sure it works with the desktop PC prior to starting ActiveSync. Another thing you need to ensure is that the Allow Serial Cable Or Infrared Connection To This COM Port check box is selected in the Connection Settings dialog box in ActiveSync. You'll also need to configure your Pocket PC for the infrared connection. To do that, tap the Start menu, and then tap Programs. Under Programs, tap the Connections folder and then tap the IR ActiveSync icon. Synchronization and connectivity will begin.

Installing ActiveSync

The installation of ActiveSync is pretty straightforward: a wizard guides you through the setup process. To install ActiveSync, follow these steps:

1. Insert the Microsoft ActiveSync 3.1 CD into your CD-ROM drive. The Setup Wizard will appear on your screen.

2. Click Next to display the Select Installation Folder screen. You can install ActiveSync in the default folder or create a new folder. Click the Change button to select a different folder for installation.

3. Click Next to display the Get Connected screen. Follow the instructions on the screen.

4. Click Next to display the Checking COM Ports screen. ActiveSync uses automated built-in mechanisms to search for the Pocket PC by looking for serial, infrared, and USB ports on the desktop PC and determining which port is active.

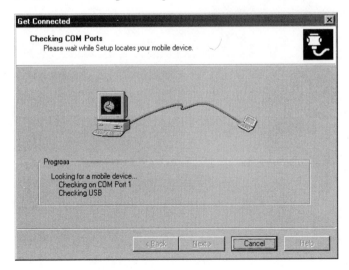

If your Pocket PC is connected to any of these ports, Active-Sync will find the device and adjust its settings accordingly. If the device is not detected, you need to configure the desktop PC to receive connection data from the Pocket PC.

5. The Set Up A Partnership screen will be displayed. The wizard will ask you whether you want to set up a partnership or connect as Guest. If you want to synchronize information between your desktop PC and the Pocket PC, select Yes to set up a partnership. If you only want to install software to the device or maybe browse the device to move files back and forth, select No.

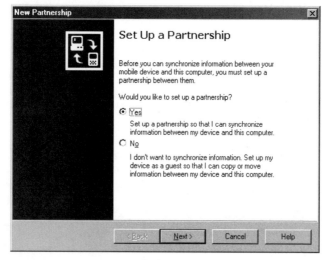

6. Click Next to display the Select Number Of Partnerships screen. If you want to synchronize with multiple computers, select synchronization with multiple computers; otherwise, select synchronization with only one PC.

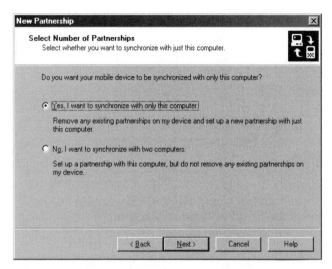

7. Click Next to display the Select Synchronization Settings screen. Choose the options you want to synchronize. (See the next section for a detailed discussion of synchronization options.)

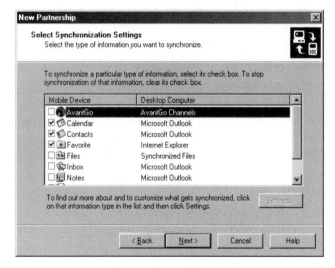

8. Click Next to display the Setup Complete screen.

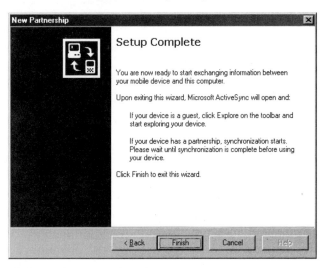

9. Click Finish to complete the setup.

Finally, the Combine Or Replace screen is displayed because ActiveSync recognizes that you have data on the Pocket PC. This screen presents you with three options: to combine the data from the device and the PC, to replace the information on the device with that on the PC, or not to synchronize the information at that time. If you have the most current data on the desktop PC, the best choice is to replace the information on the device with the information on the PC. If the data on the device is more recent, you will want to combine the data from the device and the PC. Replacing the data on the device replaces only the data that normally gets synchronized and does not delete or remove any personal documents or files from the Pocket PC.

Synchronization Options

ActiveSync allows you to synchronize more than your personal information management (PIM) items such as contacts and tasks. You can also synchronize several other types of data, including your Favorites list.

If you're synchronizing a new Pocket PC, I recommend that you select only Calendar, Contacts, and Tasks. After the synchronization of that data is complete, go back and choose other options to synchronize. Depending on how much data is on your Pocket PC, this strategy will help eliminate the time needed for the initial synchronization.

After you install ActiveSync, you can view the different synchronization options by opening ActiveSync, selecting Tools from the menu bar, and then selecting Options. You can also add or remove synchronization options after the installation of ActiveSync.

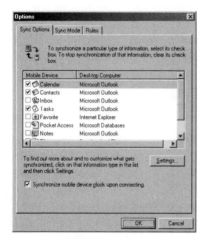

Each synchronization, or sync, option has its own settings, which you can modify. To obtain the settings information for each of the sync options, select an option and click the Settings button on the Sync Options tab of the Options screen.

The following sections cover each sync option and its settings.

Calendar

The Calendar option has three settings. The first setting synchronizes all appointments. If an appointment changes on either the desktop PC or the Pocket PC, the Calendar on the other machine is adjusted.

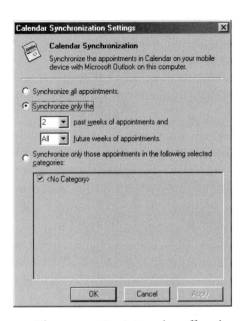

The next setting is one that offers the most opportunity for customization. Instead of synchronizing all appointments, you can opt to synchronize past appointments for one or more weeks. You can even synchronize appointments that are a specific number of weeks in the future, or you can just choose to synchronize all future weeks. Depending on the number of appointments you have, the second option might be the most useful because you can limit the amount of data you carry, and that will in turn free more memory on your device. You might want to carry data from only one week ago and one week into the future; you can accomplish this by selecting 1 Past Weeks Of Appointments And 1 Future Weeks Of Appointments.

The third setting for the Calendar synchronizes specific categories of information. Because all the synchronization for the Calendar on the Pocket PC is accomplished through Microsoft Outlook, it makes sense to take advantage of Outlook's category feature when a desktop PC is synchronized with the Pocket PC. Categories are a great way to segregate your appointments according to purpose. For example, you might have certain appointments that are work related and other appointments that are personal. You can use categories to keep these appointments separate. You can choose to synchronize only your work appointments or only your personal appointments. Synchronizing categories allows you to choose which data you want to take with you on the road. (I'll discuss categories in more detail in Chapter 10.)

Contacts

Like the Calendar, Contacts has three settings. The first setting synchronizes the complete set of contacts on the Pocket PC with the contacts on the desktop PC. The second setting synchronizes each contact selected from the list provided. The third setting synchronizes certain categories. As with Calendar categories, you can synchronize the categories that you've created in Contacts.

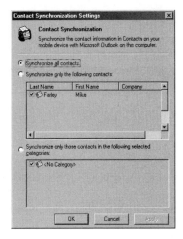

Inbox

You'll find that you have a few different ways to use e-mail on the Pocket PC. One of the obvious ways to send and receive e-mail messages is to connect your device to the Internet through a modem. Another way is to synchronize your e-mail so that when you take your Pocket PC with you, it will have the same e-mail messages as your desktop PC. To do this, leave the device in the cradle and connected to the desktop PC. When new e-mail messages arrive on the desktop PC, they'll be copied to the device through ActiveSync's automatic sync feature. You don't need to move e-mail back and forth manually.

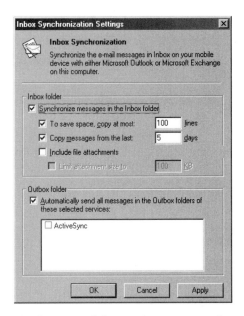

Because of the varying amount of e-mail that people receive, the options in the Inbox Synchronization Settings dialog box allow for flexibility in the way you synchronize your e-mail from the desktop PC with your Pocket PC. Because e-mail can take up a large amount of memory, you might not want to copy all of your e-mail to the Pocket PC or you might just want to get a preview of an e-mail message by copying only the first 100 lines. You can change this setting to copy more or less than 100 lines of an e-mail message.

Another setting synchronizes e-mail messages from the past five days (or a number of days that you specify). If you don't select this setting, all e-mail in the Inbox will be synchronized. A good practice is to select a number of days' worth of e-mail messages to synchronize. This will help reduce the amount of memory used on the device.

A third setting can also help reduce the strain on memory by limiting the size of e-mail attachments that are synchronized or by keeping attachments from being synchronized at all.

The bottom section of the Inbox Synchronization Settings dialog box is actually used for sending e-mail from the Outbox folder on the Pocket PC. The Pocket PC has a couple of different ways of sending e-mail. You can connect to an Internet service provider (ISP) to send and receive e-mail, or you can use ActiveSync. (See Chapter 9 for more information about sending and receiving e-mail using an ISP.)

ActiveSync allows you to create a message on the Pocket PC and send it even when the device isn't physically connected to the Internet. The message stays in the Outbox folder on the device until the Pocket PC is connected to the desktop PC and you enable synchronization. When the data is synchronized, the message in the Outbox is transferred to the desktop PC and is sent out automatically. If the Outbox weren't synchronized, the message would sit in the Outbox on the device until a connection was made to an ISP. Then the message would be sent through the ISP's mail system.

Tasks

Tasks allow you to set up simple reminders of activities that might have specific deadlines. Tasks are similar to Outlook appointments but are more simplistic.

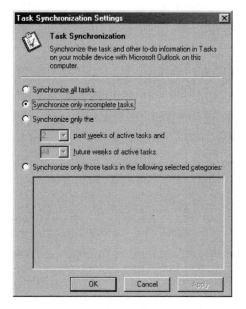

The settings for Tasks are similar to settings for Contacts and Calendar. For instance, Tasks can be synchronized according to your custom categories. One setting, however, is different for Tasks—the option to synchronize only incomplete tasks. This option might allow you to save memory by synchronizing only tasks that aren't completed instead of synchronizing all tasks.

Favorites

Up to now, I've discussed synchronizing items that are components of Outlook. Another sync option that isn't part of Outlook but is useful is the synchronization of Microsoft Internet Explorer favorites.

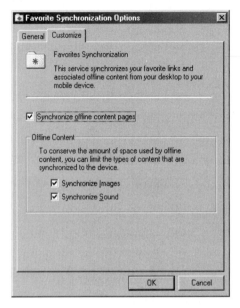

This option allows you to synchronize your favorites from Internet Explorer on the desktop PC with your Pocket PC. Using the Favorites options in ActiveSync, you can choose whether to download sounds and images to your device. If you choose not to download these items, you can save memory on the Pocket PC. Because most models of the Pocket PC have 32 MB of memory, however, conserving memory is rarely an issue. It's something that you need to pay attention to, though, especially if the performance of your Pocket PC begins to slow. (I'll discuss synchronizing favorites in more detail later in this chapter.)

Pocket Access

In the list of synchronization options for ActiveSync, you'll see a selection for Pocket Access. As you might already know, Microsoft Pocket Access isn't available for the Pocket PC. So why does ActiveSync show Pocket Access as an option? Keep in mind that ActiveSync can also be used with the Handheld PC. The Handheld PC Professional edition has Pocket Access as a built-in program. Also, from a software development perspective, Pocket Access has components that allow programmers to synchronize custom data stored on the device. Most Microsoft Windows CE programming books cover this scenario.

Notes

The Pocket PC allows you to take quick notes using the Notes program. On the desktop PC, you can create notes in Outlook just as you would on the Pocket PC. Notes provide a quick and easy way to record a snippet of information. In ActiveSync, there are no settings for Notes—just select the Notes option.

Files

Sometimes you have information that doesn't quite fit into the options that we have already talked about. Maybe you have a text file or a spreadsheet that you want to keep with you. None of the previous sync options allows you to copy these files from your desktop PC to your Pocket PC. With file synchronization, however, you can choose specific files that you want to copy to your Pocket PC, modify them, and then update the files on the desktop PC through synchronization.

With the File Synchronization settings, you can choose which files to synchronize. By clicking either the Add or the Remove button, you can easily modify the list of synchronized files. (I'll discuss synchronizing files in more detail later in this chapter.)

AvantGo

The last synchronization item listed on the SyncOptions tab is AvantGo. AvantGo is a free interactive service that offers access to personalized content and applications on the Web through the Pocket PC.

One feature of AvantGo is that every time you synchronize your Pocket PC, your device is updated dynamically with the latest information. Depending on the settings that you choose on the AvantGo server, the type of information you can get includes movie times and locations for a specific zip code and up-to-date news from the *New York Times*. (I'll discuss AvantGo in more detail later in this chapter.)

Synchronizing Internet Explorer Favorites

When you install ActiveSync, a Mobile Favorites folder is created in the Favorites folder in Internet Explorer on the desktop PC. When you see a Web site that you would like on the Pocket PC, you can choose to add it to your Mobile Favorites folder. (I'll discuss how to add a link to the Mobile Favorites folder in Chapter 8.)

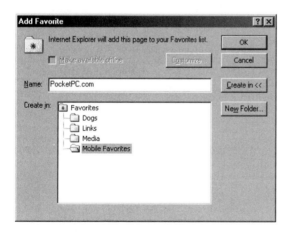

Every time you synchronize, the contents of that Web page will be added to the device. If the Web page changes, the content of the Web page is also changed on the device when Favorites are synchronized.

This is a quick method of getting Web content to the device for offline viewing. Using some of the settings in Internet Explorer, you can specify how many links deep you want to synchronize. Keep in mind that the deeper the links, the more memory the Web pages consume.

On the Pocket PC, access your Mobile Favorites by tapping the yellow folder icon on the Internet Explorer for the Pocket PC menu.

Favorites

After you synchronize Mobile Favorites, links to your favorite Web pages will show up in this folder in a tree structure. This is where you will also view your AvantGo channels. You can add or remove links from the list. Those changes will take effect on the desktop PC the next time you synchronize.

Synchronizing Files

Yes, you can manually move files from your desktop PC to your Pocket PC, but wouldn't it be nice if these files updated themselves so that the same information was in both locations? The Files option in ActiveSync allows you to configure ActiveSync to synchronize files in a specific folder on the desktop PC with the files on the Pocket PC. When you choose the File sync option, a Synchronized Files folder is created on the desktop PC.

The folder will have the name of the device followed by My Documents, such as Pocket_PC My Documents. (Pocket_PC is the name of the device.) If you want a specific document synchronized every time a change is made to it on your desktop PC, all you have to do is save it in the Synchronized Files folder. The synchronization of ActiveSync will take that document and send it to the Pocket PC.

> **Note** When you transfer files from the desktop PC to the Pocket PC or vice versa, the files are converted from one form to the other. For example, if you synchronize a Word document from the desktop PC with the Pocket PC, the file is converted to Pocket Word when it is synchronized. When this happens, some of the formatting might be lost. This isn't usually a problem, but be sure to check your documents after they are transferred.

Moving Files

File synchronization is one way to move files to and from your desktop PC and Pocket PC. The other method is drag-and-drop. If you want to move a file from your desktop PC to your Pocket PC, you can just click the Explore button in ActiveSync's toolbar to open the Mobile Device window, find the file in your desktop PC, and drag it to the Mobile Device window. You can view the contents of a device if the device is attached to a desktop PC in the Mobile Device window.

Working with AvantGo Content

Most Web sites are designed with the desktop PC in mind. Web designers don't give too much consideration to devices with smaller screens and limited memory. Some Web site designers are starting to tailor the content on their sites to be user-friendly for Internet Explorer for the Pocket PC. This usually means reducing the size of graphics and pages to match the screen sizes of the Pocket PC. AvantGo delivers this properly formatted information directly to your Pocket PC.

AvantGo uses ActiveSync and Internet Explorer for the Pocket PC to view the content on the device. Using ActiveSync, AvantGo content is brought to the device by an Internet connection to the AvantGo Web site (*http://www.avantgo.com*). If you want to receive content from the AvantGo Web site, you need to be a registered user. Once you register, choose the type of information that you would like to receive. After you've chosen the type of information for which you want to receive regular updates, synchronize your device. To receive the most current information from the AvantGo server, you must be connected to the Internet when synchronizing. Keep in mind that the information you choose to receive is customized to fit the screen of the Pocket PC, without the need for scrolling or any customization on your part. And after you synchronize, the most current AvantGo content is downloaded to the device, making for a completely mobile Internet experience.

Configuring AvantGo in ActiveSync the first time can be a little confusing. In ActiveSync, you must have the AvantGo option selected. Then you need to configure AvantGo with your username and password by following these steps:

1. Click the Settings button on the Sync Options tab of the Options dialog box to open the Mobile Link dialog box.

2. Click the Properties button to open the Edit Server Profile dialog box.

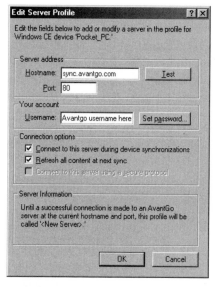

3. In the Your Account section, enter the username that you established when you registered on the AvantGo Web site.

4. Click the Set Password button, and enter the password that you established on the AvantGo Web site.

5. Click OK three times to complete the configuration.

The next time you synchronize your Pocket PC, the subscribed information will be synchronized with the device.

On the Pocket PC, the AvantGo content is stored in the Favorites area of Internet Explorer for the Pocket PC. To access Favorites, tap the folder icon at the bottom of the Internet Explorer for the Pocket PC window and then tap AvantGo Channels. You should see the content that you subscribed to.

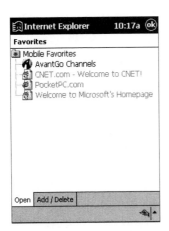

To organize your content or to add or remove selections from Avant-Go, just log in to the AvantGo Web site and select or deselect the content you want to change. The next time you are connected to the Internet and you synchronize, the changes will be made on the Pocket PC.

What if you're in a corporate environment and you synchronize AvantGo content through a proxy server? AvantGo allows you to use a proxy server if necessary to synchronize your information.

> **Note** A *proxy server* is a computer that is connected to the Internet that allows several other machines on the network to access the Internet. It submits Internet requests by several users.

To configure AvantGo to work with a proxy server, in the Mobile Link dialog box click the Connection tab. This window has two buttons: Change and Autodetect Now. You can click Autodetect Now, which will attempt to search for the type of connection you have and then configure itself accordingly. The other option is to manually configure the connection by clicking the Change button and entering the proxy settings necessary for your network. If you don't know your settings, check with your system administrator.

Troubleshooting

I'd like to say that we live in a perfect world when it comes to software and how it interacts with other software, but that's not the case. After being in a software product support department for a few years, I can tell you that sometimes software—and even hardware—can have a mind of its own. Because of the thousands of hardware and software configurations possible on Pocket PCs and desktop systems, it's almost inevitable that you will run into a problem at some point when you're synchronizing data. In case you do have a problem, here are a few remedies. Try one remedy, and then try to synchronize again.

- Reset the Pocket PC. Two resets are available in the Pocket PC—soft reset and hard reset. In this case, do a soft reset. This is similar to rebooting your desktop PC.

- Be sure that the cable that you're using for synchronization is in place. Check the cable connection to both the device and the desktop PC. If your Pocket PC synchronizes fine one day and not the next, a loose or improperly connected cable is often the culprit.

- Select the appropriate connection settings in the Connections Settings dialog box in ActiveSync. Ensure that the correct COM port is selected and that the Allow Serial Cable Or Infrared Connection To This COM Port check box is selected. If you're using a USB-enabled device, be sure that Allow USB Connection With This Desktop Computer is also selected.

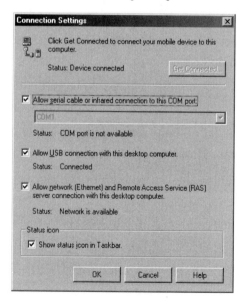

■ Delete the partnership. Each Pocket PC that connects to Active-Sync is associated with a partnership. The partnership information is stored in the registry of the desktop PC. To delete the partnership, disconnect the Pocket PC from its cable. Then open ActiveSync, and on the File menu select Delete Partnership to display the Confirm Partnership Deletion dialog box. Tap Yes, and the Confirm Folder Deletion dialog box will be displayed. You'll be asked whether you want to delete the Synchronized Files folder. Tap Yes if you're not synchronizing files and don't have files in the Synchronized Files folder in My Documents. Otherwise, select No. The partnership is then deleted.

■ Re-create the partnership. To re-create the partnership, you will need to run the Get Connected Wizard from the file menu in ActiveSync. The wizard will redetect your Pocket PC and begin to set up a new partnership. If you are using a laptop with an infrared port and are trying to connect your Pocket PC using a serial connection, the resources of the serial port might be allocated to the infrared port. To reallocate the resources to the serial port, open the CMOS of the laptop, disable the infrared port, and then enable the serial port. You might need to consult your laptop's documentation for instructions on changing your CMOS settings.

> **Warning**   Keep in mind that you can accidentally change settings within the CMOS that could make your machine unbootable. Be careful!

■ If you receive an "unresolved items" message, use ActiveSync's Resolve Items tool, which you can find in the ActiveSync Tools menu. This tool allows you to select the item to resolve and choose how to resolve it. For example, you might have a contact, appointment, or task that is a duplicate. ActiveSync gives you the option of choosing which one to keep.

Summing Up

ActiveSync is an extremely useful component that works in conjunction with the Pocket PC. Not only does ActiveSync synchronize your most essential information from Outlook, but it can also make the Pocket PC a customizable device with several methods of taking content with you on the go. With Favorites synchronization and AvantGo, you can take the Internet with you—right in your pocket.

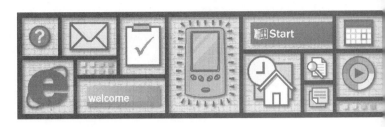

4

Getting Connected

It's finally here—the Internet in the palm of your hand. As the Internet becomes more mainstream, we've come to depend on it for everything from news updates to grocery shopping. And the growing popularity of portable computing devices has paved the way for the Internet to become an extension of these devices.

The handheld computer emerged from advances in the miniaturization of technology, but until quite recently, the handheld computer wasn't much more than a calculator or an electronic appointment book. Now it contains many of the same features found on a desktop PC 15 times its size. Functionality such as Web browsing and accessing and sending e-mail make the handheld computing device comparable to a full-size PC.

Using Your ISP to Connect

Currently the most popular way to access the Internet is by using an Internet service provider (ISP) such as Earthlink, America Online (AOL), or MSN to connect the computing device to a phone line or a wireless connection. (I'll discuss wireless connections in Chapter 7.)

The Pocket PC can connect to almost all available ISPs. If the ISP uses industry-standard technologies, chances are the Pocket PC can connect. If the ISP or the destination computer is not using technology that is popular within the industry, however, the Pocket PC might have difficulty connecting.

To connect your Pocket PC to an ISP, the ISP must support either Point-to-Point Protocol (PPP) and Transfer Control Protocol/Internet Protocol (TCP/IP) or Serial Line Internet Protocol (SLIP) and TCP/IP. PPP and SLIP are two communication protocols that allow a computer connected to a server via a modem to become an extension of the connecting network. These are the same protocols that are supported in the desktop version of Microsoft Windows.

TCP/IP is the language of the Internet—the language computers connected to the Internet use to communicate with each other. Any computer that wants to communicate on the Internet needs a distinct address that will identify it to any other computer. This address is called an Internet Protocol (IP) address, and it's one of the components that allow you to browse the Web and send or receive e-mail.

Usually when you make a connection to an ISP, you are given an IP address while you use that ISP's server. Using this IP address is also known as "leasing" it. When you disconnect from the ISP, your lease expires. The next time you log in, you might be given the same IP address or you might be given a new one. Some ISPs might give you a specific IP address for your use alone. This static IP address does not change; it is your unique identifier on the Internet. Most ISPs rarely assign a static IP address. You are usually given a dynamic IP address that is different each time you log in.

> **Note** This discussion about TCP/IP gives only a brief insight into TCP/IP and how it works with the Pocket PC. Several books about TCP/IP are available, in case you want more in-depth information than covered here.

What You Need for an ISP Connection

The Pocket PC comes with all the software you need to connect to another computer or to an ISP. If your Pocket PC doesn't have a built-in modem, the only item you'll need to obtain separately is a modem. Most modems are CompactFlash (CF) and work easily with the CF slot on the device. All modems available in CF size are 56 Kbps in speed. In addition to the modem, you will need an account with an ISP. You can probably use the same ISP that you use for your desktop PC, making it convenient to receive your e-mail at either location.

After you insert the modem into the CF slot on the device, the system recognizes the modem. Be aware that the system won't indicate that it recognizes the modem until you walk through the steps of connecting to the ISP.

Connecting to Your ISP: Step by Step

Once you've inserted the modem into the Pocket PC, you can walk through the steps of connecting to an ISP. This process is essentially the same as setting up a connection with Windows 98 on a desktop PC. After you have gone through these steps once, you won't need to go through them again the next time you want to connect to the Internet. These steps might seem a little complicated, but the plethora of connection options to ISPs and remote computers makes it difficult to come up with a common method of connecting for every computing device every time.

To create an ISP connection, follow these steps:

1. Tap Start, then tap Settings, and then tap the Connections tab.

2. Tap the Modem icon.

3. From the list of modem connections, tap New Connection.

4. On the Make New Connection screen, enter the name of your connection. This name identifies the connection that you are making. For example, you might want to call your connection "RAS Connection" or "Earthlink."

5. From the list of modems, select the type of modem that you inserted into your Pocket PC.

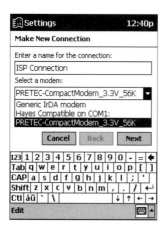

Note If your modem does not show up in the list, you might need to reseat the modem by removing it and reinserting it into the device. If the modem still does not show up in the list, consult your modem manufacturer to see whether other software is needed to operate your modem. You can also try the selection Hayes Compatible On COM1.

6. Next set the baud rate to a supported rate for your modem. If you don't see a baud rate that matches that of your modem, choose the next-highest rate. For example, if you have a 56K modem, choose 57600 from the list.

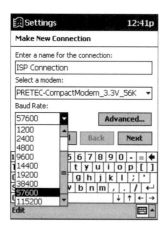

> **Note** Under most circumstances, you don't need to modify any settings under the Advanced button. However, if you want to make any changes to these settings, refer to the sidebar "The Advanced Settings" on the next page.

7. Tap Next to display the ISP Connection screen. This screen allows you to enter the country code, area code, and phone number of the computer you want to dial.

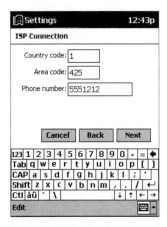

8. Tap Next. The final screen allows you to customize extra settings that might be needed for your connection. To be specific, you can set connection timeout time; you can also specify whether you want to wait for a dial tone before dialing. This setting comes in handy when you have voice mail on your phone line. A beeping dial tone or other signal will indicate that you have a message. Waiting for a dial tone allows the modem to begin dialing only after the voice mail signal ends. You can also specify how many seconds you want to wait before dialing with a credit card. In addition, you can add extra dialing commands to the modem. This is a rarely used setting. If modem strings are necessary, you need to locate those strings from your modem manufacturer.

9. Tap Finish, and you've created your connection.

The Advanced Settings

You can change the Advanced settings on the Advanced screen, which is displayed after you tap Advanced on the Make New Connection screen. This screen has three tabs: Port Settings, TCP/IP, and Name Servers.

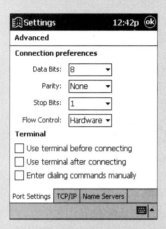

The Port Settings tab controls settings for data bits, parity, stop bits, and so on. In the Terminal section of this tab, you can select the use of a terminal before a connection is established or after a connection is established. If your ISP requires you to manually enter a dialing command, select the Enter Dialing Commands Manually box. You might need to use some of these settings when dialing in to a corporate server or to an older ISP that uses other forms of connections. If you don't know whether you should use these settings, consult your system administrator or ISP.

If you have a specific IP address, you can enter that on the TCP/IP tab. Most ISPs and corporate organizations dynamically assign an address when you connect. The default TCP/IP setting under Advanced is Use Server-Assigned IP Address. This means that the ISP will give you a dynamic address when you connect. You might not have that address the next time you connect. The other option is Use Specific IP Address. When you select this option, you need to enter an IP address assigned by your ISP when you signed up originally.

The other settings on the TCP/IP tab (Use Slip, Use Software Compression, and Use IP Header Compression) are dependent on your ISP. Your ISP or system administrator should have this information.

Under the Name Servers tab, you have the option of entering IP addresses for Domain Name System (DNS) and Windows Internet Names Service (WINS) servers. Again, this is a setting that is specific to your ISP. Some ISPs dynamically set your DNS servers for you, so you never have to enter any DNS entries. The DNS and WINS servers translate names such as www.microsoft.com to IP addresses. When you type an address for a Web site, you are actually telling the computer to find an IP address. Servers on the Internet take the "friendly" name and translate it to an IP address so that data can be sent back to you. These servers are DNS servers.

(continued)

The Advanced Settings *continued*
There are usually two DNS servers: DNS and Alt DNS. The Alt DNS is used when the main DNS is not functioning. The WINS servers are used the same way DNS servers are used except that you find WINS servers on a corporate network.

Note If you are having trouble browsing the Web and you have verified that your settings are correct, you might want to make sure the DNS server is responding. If you can go to a Web site by using the IP address and not the friendly name, the DNS server is down. You can use any DNS server on the Web; you don't have to specifically use the DNS server from your ISP. In fact, you can use a DNS server from another ISP. To find DNS servers, do a Web search for the words *DNS servers*.

Making the Connection

The following steps allow you to initiate a connection:

1. Tap Start, then tap Programs, and then tap Connections.

2. In the Connections folder, you will see all the connection settings that you just created. Tap the connection that you created with the previous steps.

Getting Connected   Chapter 4

3. Now you need to enter your username and password. If you are dialing the same ISP that you use for your desktop PC, enter the same username and password. If you want to avoid entering your password each time, select the Save Password check box. Selecting this box is not advised if you allow other people to use your device because they could connect to your ISP and get your credentials without knowing your password.

> **Note** In a corporate environment you usually need to provide one more piece of information: the domain. The domain field allows a user to be authenticated against the domain. That means that the corporate network validates your username and password against a complex set of rules, usually on a Microsoft Windows NT server network. If you are unsure whether your network requires a domain, consult your system administrator.

4. Verify that the phone number is correct. If the phone number is incorrect, tap Dialing Options, make the necessary changes, and then tap OK to close the Dialing Options screen. We'll discuss changing dialing options in detail later in this chapter.

> **Note** Some ISPs require special commands to get connected to their service. For example, MSN requires that you enter MSN/ in front of your username.

49

> **Note** If your ISP is AOL, you will need to install the AOL client application if it is not installed already. You can obtain the client from a supplemental CD-ROM packaged with your Pocket PC. After you install the client, you will not need to follow the steps in this section. The AOL software handles all your connection settings for you.

5. Tap Connect. The modem will try to dial the number that you specified.

During the process, you probably won't hear the modem noises that you hear when making a connection with your desktop PC. You will, however, be able to watch status notifications on the Pocket PC screen. These notifications let you know what is happening during the connection process. When you're connected, you'll hear a distinctive tone from the Pocket PC and a message will appear on the screen stating that you are connected. Once you're connected, you can use Internet Explorer to browse the Web and send or receive e-mail. (I'll discuss these features in Chapters 8 and 9.)

Adjusting ISP Connection Settings

If you follow the steps in the previous section, you will connect to your ISP successfully. However, as I mentioned earlier, not all ISPs are the same. You might need to adjust settings the first few times that you connect. To make adjustments to the settings, follow these steps:

1. Tap Start, then tap Programs, and then tap Connections.

2. Tap and hold your stylus on the connection you created for two seconds. You will then be presented with a submenu with the Edit menu item.

3. Choose Edit to display your ISP connection screen, where you can adjust your ISP connection settings.

Ending the Connection

Once the connection is established, you can disconnect it by following these steps:

1. Go to the Today screen.

2. Tap the icon in the lower right corner that resembles two small computers to display the Connect To screen. This screen has two buttons: Disconnect and Hide Status.

3. Tapping Hide Status minimizes that window. Tapping Disconnect will disconnect the modem from the phone line and terminate your connection to the ISP or remote computer.

Changing Dialing Options

Dialing Options is an area that you won't have to change much except for a little fine-tuning. Why would you want to change the dialing options? Typically, you'll change your dialing options when you've changed the location you're calling from.

For example, you might have one location established for your place of employment and another location set for you home. Both use the same phone number to dial your ISP, but they might be in different area codes.

There are also settings to disable call waiting and to change dialing patterns. These come in handy when you need to customize your calling string. For example, you might need to dial a 9 for an outside line. Or maybe you need to pause the modem after dialing the 9 to get a dial tone. Inserting a comma in the dialing string forces a fixed 2-second delay before dialing. There is no limit to the number of commas you can use to increase the delay time.

Summing Up

Getting connected with the Pocket PC is an essential feature of the device, allowing you to browse the Web and send and receive e-mail. In this chapter, you learned what you need to get connected and how to set up the initial connection, including configuring your username and password. You learned about connecting to ISPs and remote computers, such as a corporate network server. In the next chapter, you'll learn how to make a wireless connection with your Pocket PC.

5

Remote Synchronization with a Modem

Much of the time we are mobile, and portable computing devices allow us to make the most efficient use of our time. However, we are still somewhat dependent on our desktop PCs because they keep receiving fresh and updated information. Using a modem to connect to the network that your PC is connected to lets you stay current with the data source that you usually synchronize with, even when you are away from your PC. For example, you can dial in to your PC or the network that your PC is connected to and synchronize your data, downloading the most current information to your Pocket PC. Remote synchronization, or remote sync, also works in the other direction: If you've changed the data on your Pocket PC, you can use remote sync to download that information to your desktop PC.

Remote Synchronization Layout

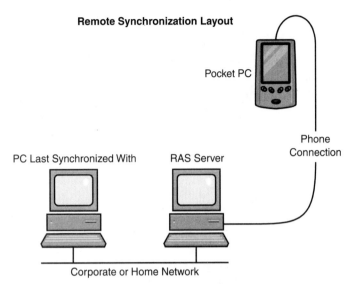

Pocket PC

Phone
Connection

PC Last Synchronized With   RAS Server

Corporate or Home Network

Let's say you're on a business trip in Miami. Before you left your office in Seattle, you synchronized your Pocket PC with your work desktop PC for the latest information. While you're out on the road, you make several important business contacts. You can use your Pocket PC to record the contact information and then dial in to your company and synchronize back with your desktop PC.

What if you're not in a company network environment? You can still use remote sync. Home networks are becoming increasingly popular. You can set up a private server to accept calls and synchronize content back with your home PC. You can do this with either a remote access server (RAS) or a dial-up server connection.

What You Need for Remote Sync with a Modem

Before you create a modem connection, you need to get from your system administrator the dial-up access telephone number, username, password, and domain name. If your Pocket PC doesn't have a built-in modem, insert a modem card into the CF slot on the device. Refer to Chapter 2 for details regarding how to choose a modem for your Pocket PC.

Setting Up Remote Sync

Setting up remote sync using a modem is fairly easy. All you really need to do on the Pocket PC is create a dial-up connection and then configure that connection to dial in to a server that can accept calls from an outside computer. The following steps illustrate remote sync setup using a modem:

1. On the Pocket PC, tap Start, tap Settings, and then tap the Connections tab at the bottom of the screen.

2. Tap Modem, and then tap New Connection.

3. Provide a name for the connection, and select the appropriate modem from the drop-down list.

> **Note**   If the modem doesn't appear in the drop-down list, check the modem connection.

4. Select the appropriate baud rate for the modem that you have. If the exact baud rate isn't listed for your modem, choose the next-highest rate. For example, if you have a 56K modem, select 57600.

5. Tap Next.

6. Enter the phone number of the PC that you are going to call.

7. Tap Next. Leave the default settings on this screen, and tap Finish.

8. Tap OK.

You now have the necessary components set up to dial in to a server for remote sync. You need to set this up only once, and you will have these settings for use at any time. The following steps initiate the actual synchronization:

9. Tap Start, tap Programs, and then tap Connections.

10. Tap ActiveSync.

11. From the drop-down list in the ActiveSync window, select the name of the connection that you just created.

12. The Connect To box contains the name of the machine that the Pocket PC last synchronized with using a cable.

> **Note** The name of the machine is the most important part of this window. If this name is not the machine that you last synchronized with, you will need to physically go to the machine that you want to synchronize with and synchronize. The proper machine name should then show up in the Connect To box.

13. Tap Connect.

14. Enter your username and password if you have not done so already. Enter the domain if that is required in your environment.

15. Confirm that the phone number is correct. If it is not correct, tap Dialing Options and correct the phone number.

16. Tap Connect. Once you're connected, you will be notified of the number of items that are out-of-date.

17. Proceed with synchronizing by tapping Sync Now.

If you want to set up RAS to accept calls from an outside source, you might need to contact your system administrator or consult further documentation on the subject. The Microsoft Knowledge Base is a good source of information. The following links will take you to articles regarding setting up dial-in access on Microsoft Windows 98 and Windows 2000:

- For Windows 98: *http://support.microsoft.com/support/kb/articles/ Q139/7/10.asp?LN=EN-US&SD=gn&FR=0*

- For Windows 2000: *http://support.microsoft.com/support/kb/ articles/Q254/3/16.ASP?LN=EN-US&SD=gn&FR=0*

Troubleshooting Remote Sync with a Modem

Problems with remote sync using a modem usually occur after the Pocket PC has made a connection and is trying to find the PC that it last synchronized with. To sync with the proper PC, that PC needs to be on the network and turned on. It does not need to be logged in to the network.

Depending on the layout of the network, problems can occur when the PC you want to synchronize with is on a different subnet or on the other side of a misconfigured router. Contact your system administrator if you suspect a layout like this.

Before traveling with your Pocket PC, be sure to check that remote synchronization works. Troubleshooting remote synchronization is more difficult from the road because you can't access the dial-in server. Before you leave, be sure that you can dial in to the server and that you can access the machine you normally sync with across the network.

Summing Up

Remote sync with a modem is just one of the many ways you can retrieve your data while you're on the road. All you need is a Pocket PC, a modem, and a server that can accept incoming calls. With this combination, you can retrieve the most current information from the office and you can send the most current updates from the road back to the office, and your data will always stay fresh. In the next chapter, I will discuss how to perform remote sync via Ethernet.

6

Remote Synchronization via Ethernet

This chapter does not necessarily pertain to every Pocket PC user, but if you're a corporate user and you want to synchronize across an Ethernet connection, you'll find helpful information here.

As you will see in this book, there are many ways to receive data with your Pocket PC. Of course, you might not need to use all these options, but you'll probably find some of them quite useful.

Ethernet synchronization, or Ethernet sync, is one of those options. If you work in a corporate environment, your desktop PC is probably connected to a network of other computers. The network allows people to access and share information. The corporate network is a private network available only to corporate employees. It's usually faster and more secure than the public network (the Internet).

The most common corporate network type is Ethernet, which is usually used in high-speed networks and is easily scalable to the number of users who are on the network. Ethernet is the most popular network architecture for local area networks (LANs). A LAN is a small network, such as the network in a corporate building or the network that you might have in your place of employment.

Using Ethernet Sync

Let's say you work in a large organization that has a network of computers connecting everybody over a distance of several miles between buildings. Let's also say that you have meetings in several of the buildings farthest from your office. Separated by such a distance, you might find it difficult to retrieve your data from your desktop PC back in your office. You could lug along a laptop and use that to get your e-mail and latest meeting requests, or you could use your Pocket PC to quickly get the information you need without the extra boot time and space a laptop necessitates. By connecting your Pocket PC to the Ethernet network, you can retrieve the latest information from your PC back in your office.

What You Need for Ethernet Sync

To use Ethernet sync, you'll typically need three items: an Ethernet card, a network cable, and, of course, a Pocket PC.

The Pocket PC doesn't come with an Ethernet card; you'll have to purchase this separately. The speed at which you can synchronize with the Ethernet card makes it a valuable investment. Most Pocket PCs offer expandability through a CompactFlash (CF) slot, so you'll need to purchase a CF Ethernet card. These are easy to find at most computer retail stores.

Configuring Your Pocket PC for Ethernet Sync

One feature of the Pocket PC is the ability to automatically recognize a hardware component when it is inserted into the CompactFlash slot. This makes using multiple CF devices easy. When you insert a CF Ethernet card into the Pocket PC, the Pocket PC recognizes it and if necessary starts the proper network configuration software. From there, you can initiate Microsoft ActiveSync on the Pocket PC to synchronize across the network. As with remote synchronization using a modem, you must first have a connection on the network before you start ActiveSync. (See Chapter 5 for information about remote synchronization using a modem.) In contrast with remote synchronization with a modem, there is no need to create a dial-up connection. You might, however, need to configure a few settings, as illustrated by the following steps:

1. Use a cable, cradle, or infrared connection to establish a partnership between the Pocket PC and your PC.
2. Disconnect the Pocket PC from your PC.

3. Insert the CF Ethernet card into the Pocket PC. If you receive a message about using the card while the Pocket PC is on battery power, select Yes. (If you select No, power from the Pocket PC will not be used to power the CF card and the CF card will not function.)

4. Use a network cable to connect the CF Ethernet card to the network.

5. Tap Start, tap Settings, and then select the Connections tab.

6. Tap the Network icon.

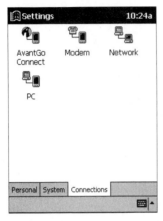

7. Tap the Identification tab at the bottom of the Network Connections screen, and enter your appropriate username, password, and domain for the network you are trying to synchronize across.

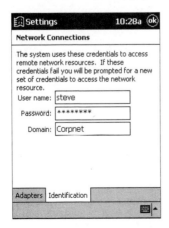

8. Tap the Adapters tab. Tap your CF adapter in the list of adapters to view or change its properties.

> **Note**   Ideally, an adapter in the list will match the CF card that you're using. If your adapter is not in the list, try the default NE2000 Compatible Ethernet Driver.

9. Enter the appropriate information for the IP Address tab and the Name Servers tab, or leave the default settings.

> **Note**   You might need to consult your system administrator for the proper settings.

10. Tap OK three times to complete the settings configuration.

Your Pocket PC should now be configured for an Ethernet connection to the network and be ready to (for example) browse the Internet with Microsoft Internet Explorer for the Pocket PC. See Chapter 8 for a detailed discussion about using the Pocket PC to browse the Internet.

Setting Up Ethernet Sync

Follow these steps to synchronize across the network using a CF Ethernet card:

1. Tap Start, tap Programs, and then tap Connections.

2. Tap ActiveSync.

3. From the drop-down list in the ActiveSync window, select the name of the connection that will connect you to the appropriate server. In this case, the connection is called Network Connection.

4. The Connect To box contains the name of the machine that the Pocket PC last synchronized with using a cable.

> **Note** The name of the machine is the most important part of this window. If this name is not the machine that you last synchronized with and it is not in the drop-down list, you will need to physically go to the machine that you want to synchronize with, and synchronize locally. The proper machine name should then show up in the Connect To box.

5. Tap Connect to display the Connecting To Desktop screen. After checking the partnership with the computer that you last synchronized with, the Pocket PC shows the Connection Status screen.

6. Tap Sync Now, and the synchronization starts between the computer and your Pocket PC.

Troubleshooting Ethernet Sync

Ethernet sync rarely presents problems, but there are a few items that you might need to look out for. You might find that you are unable to connect to your PC in your office. Several situations can cause this:

- Depending on the network layout, physical objects such as routers might not be configured properly. Consult your system administrator for possible solutions.

- There might be a name server issue, in which case you won't be able to find your desktop PC because of an incorrect Domain Name System (DNS) or Windows Internet Names Service (WINS) setting. You can correct this by confirming the appropriate settings with your system administrator. Refer to Chapter 4 for detailed discussions of DNS and WINS.

- If you are using static Internet Protocol (IP) addresses, you might be using an IP address that is already in use or is part of a different subnet. If you suspect this, consult your system administrator.

Summing Up

If you're looking for a synchronizing solution in a corporate environment, Ethernet synchronization is your answer. Your desktop PC is still the repository for most of your information, but with a CF Ethernet card and a connection to the corporate LAN, using your Pocket PC to stay current with your desktop PC is easy and fast.

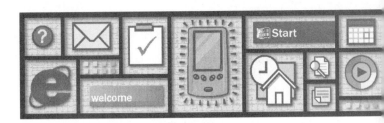

7

Going Wireless

The information we've covered so far demonstrates how the Internet has pushed its way into our lives. Now, with wireless connections, the Internet is about to become an even more prominent presence. Making wireless connections with portable devices is the next big phase in the information age. In this chapter, I'll discuss the different wireless technologies you can use to connect your Pocket PC to the Internet.

Wireless computing devices currently work from existing wireless networks. Those networks are usually the same networks that you use with your cellular phone. Cellular networks in the United States are different from those in other countries, which makes finding a common wireless solution more difficult. In the future this probably won't be an issue, but right now it is less expensive for service providers to use the existing cellular networks than it is to build new systems.

What You Get with Wireless

Wireless connectivity doesn't usually have the same functionality as a 56K modem connection. Speeds are far slower and probably cumbersome for a lot of computing activities.

As you know, the Pocket PC can browse the Web and send and receive e-mail over a modem connection. It can function the same way over a wireless connection, but much more slowly. You can still browse the Web, send and receive e-mail, and even use Microsoft ActiveSync on the Pocket PC to synchronize your data over a wireless connection. Be prepared, however, to wait for your data. As new data networks are built, connection speeds will increase.

Available Technologies for Wireless

Going wireless with the Pocket PC requires a little understanding of the wireless technologies available. It is not yet as simple as going to your local cellular retail store and saying, "I want to have a wireless Pocket PC." Understanding the technology discussed in this section can help you to determine the right wireless solution for you.

Cellular networks are the primary data providers for wireless connections. One of the more popular technologies in the United States is Cellular Digital Packet Data (CDPD). AT&T and Verizon are two companies that use this technology. CDPD supports data speeds up to 19.2 Kbps. (That's quite a difference from your 56K modem!)

Another technology that is provided by Sprint and Verizon is Code Division Multiple Access (CDMA). CDMA offers data speeds up to 14.4 Kbps and is widely available in many metropolitan areas.

A third technology to be aware of is Global Systems for Mobile Communications (GSM). In the United States, GSM is primarily used by VoiceStream and has a data rate up to 14.4 Kbps. Although GSM is the most widely used technology throughout the rest of the world, a GSM phone from the United States probably won't work in other parts of the world because of different frequencies of GSM.

A fourth technology, provided by Metricom, is the Ricochet wireless network. This network allows connections of 128 Kbps in 21 major cities in the United States. Visit Metricom's Web site at *http://www.ricochet.net* to find the current coverage areas.

Hardware Needed for Wireless

When it comes to wireless connectivity, several hardware options are available for your Pocket PC. The options I describe in this section are a few of the most popular. Since wireless connectivity is so hot, more options will undoubtedly be available in the near future. As you'll see, various forms of wireless solutions are available for the Pocket PC, and each has its own set of pros and cons. Choosing the right form might seem daunting. To determine the right wireless solution, you need to investigate the coverage available in your area. Then you must decide which hardware component you need in order to work with the wireless provider in your area. In other words, you need to make sure that your device is compatible with the wireless solution you choose.

Some cell phone models contain an infrared port that can be used for communication with the Pocket PC. To make a connection to the Internet, all you have to do is align the infrared port on the Pocket PC with the infrared port on the cell phone. The phone makes the connection and then passes data back and forth with the Pocket PC over the infrared connection. The infrared connection works great for connecting and synchronizing, but it does not offer a great solution for Web browsing. The nature of infrared requires the cell phone and the Pocket PC to remain aligned with each other and at a distance of not more than six inches. Placing both the Pocket PC and the cell phone on a flat surface works best. While data is being transmitted, the two devices cannot be moved, or the connection will be lost. This makes browsing the Web relatively difficult. However, infrared does work well for quickly synchronizing your data by using ActiveSync. Once your data is synchronized, you can disconnect and review your newly synchronized content.

Socket Communications produces a CompactFlash (CF) digital phone card with a cable. Using this card, a cell phone can make a wireless connection with the Pocket PC. You can plug the CF card into the CF slot on the Pocket PC and connect the other end of the cable to the cell phone. However, not all cell phones are compatible with this method. To find out whether your cell phone can be used with a digital phone card, check out the Socket Communications Web site at *http://www.socketcom.com*. (See the Digital Phone Card section under the Wireless Solutions section.)

Nextcell, Inc., offers a CF wireless modem card that works with CDPD networks. Called the Pocket Spider, this low-power modem card works with any Pocket PC with a PC slot. For more information on the Nextcell Pocket Spider, visit the Nextcell Web site at *http://www.nextcell.com.*

Another wireless hardware alternative is the Sierra Wireless card. This card is a PCMCIA card. A PCMCIA card is about twice the size of a CompactFlash card. Only one Pocket PC device can accept a card of this size—the Compaq iPaq Pocket PC. With the addition of the PCMCIA expansion jacket, the iPaq is capable of accepting different PCMCIA cards. The Sierra Wireless card works with existing wireless services such as AT&T, Verizon, and Ricochet networks. It is one of the fastest wireless solutions, with one of its cards offering 128 Kbps on Ricochet networks. Sierra Wireless also has a card for the AT&T and Verizon CDPD networks offering 19.2 Kbps. For more information on Sierra Wireless cards, visit the Sierra Wireless Web site at *http://www.sierrawireless.com*.

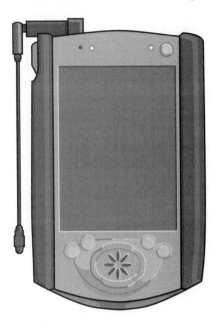

Configuring Your Pocket PC for a Wireless Connection

Once you've chosen your carrier for wireless data, you need to configure the Pocket PC for the hardware that supports the carrier. In most cases, configuring the Pocket PC for a wireless connection is similar to configuring it for a regular modem connection. You'll follow many of the same steps if you're using a Socket digital phone card.

The following steps will create a wireless connection with infrared or with a Socket digital phone card. Note that these steps will not work for configuring either the Sierra Wireless card or the Nextcell CF modem. For information on how to configure these cards with the Pocket PC, consult either the Sierra Wireless or the Nextcell Web site, or see the directions that come with these cards.

Note Even though this method of connection is wireless, you still need to connect to an Internet service provider (ISP).

---

1. Tap Start, tap Settings, and then tap the Connections tab.

2. Tap the Modem icon.

3. From the list of modem connections, tap New Connection.

4. In the Make New Connection screen, enter the name of your connection. This name identifies the connection you're making. For example, you might want to call this connection Wireless.

5. From the list of modems, select the type of modem that you inserted into your Pocket PC.

Note If you're making an infrared connection to your mobile phone, all you need to do is select Generic IrDA Modem from the drop-down list. All the other steps in this process are the same for infrared, wireless, or regular modem connections.

---

6. Now you need to set the baud rate to a supported rate for your modem. Since the given baud rates from the list don't usually match the baud rates of the modems, you typically choose the next-highest rate. The default baud rate, 19200, is probably a safe choice for most wireless networks.

Note Under most circumstances, you don't need to modify any settings under the Advanced button. However, if you want to make any changes to these settings, refer to the sidebar "The Advanced Settings" in Chapter 6.

7. Tap Next to display the ISP Connection screen. This screen allows you to enter the country code, area code, and phone number of the computer you are trying to dial.

8. Tap Next. The final screen allows you to customize extra settings that might be needed for your connection. The first setting allows you to set an amount of time to wait before connection failure will cause a timeout. The second setting allows you to wait for a dial tone before dialing. (This setting comes in handy if you sometimes have the "broken" dial tone associated with voice mail on your phone line.) The third setting tells the modem to wait a certain amount of time before dialing with a credit card. The last setting in this section allows you to add extra commands to the modem when it dials a number. This is a rarely used setting; if you need modem strings, get them from your modem manufacturer.

9. Tap Finish.

Your Pocket PC is now ready to make a connection to your ISP. Make sure the digital phone card is in the Pocket PC and the cable is attached to the cell phone. You might also need to place your cell phone in a special data-transmission mode. If so, you will need to consult the documentation that comes with the phone or your phone manufacturer.

The following steps will initiate a wireless connection to your ISP:

1. Tap Start, tap Programs, and then tap Connections.

2. In the Connections folder, you will see all the connection settings you just created. Tap the connection that you created in the preceding steps.

3. Enter your username and password. If you are dialing the same ISP that you use for your desktop PC, enter the same username and password.

4. Verify that the phone number is correct. If the phone number is incorrect, tap Dialing Options, make the necessary changes, and then tap OK to close the Dialing Options screen.

5. Tap Connect.

Summing Up

Many options for mobile computing with wireless connectivity are available, and they are changing rapidly. What is popular today won't necessarily be popular tomorrow. You have several options for wireless connectivity: Socket digital phone cards, Nextcell modem cards, and Sierra Wireless cards. In the coming years, wireless technology will evolve so much that we will undoubtedly look back at today's options and laugh at the slow speeds.

8

Exploring the Web with the Pocket PC

You've learned the different methods of connecting to the Internet with your Pocket PC. Now let's talk about the tool you will probably use the most while you are connected: Microsoft Internet Explorer for the Pocket PC. This program allows you to surf the Web just like you do on your desktop PC. Internet Explorer for the Pocket PC has the capability to browse almost any Web site on the Internet.

What Does Internet Explorer for the Pocket PC Support?

Limited storage and screen size prevent Internet Explorer for the Pocket PC from supporting everything that your desktop PC version supports. The following table lists the terms that will allow you to identify what is supported on Internet Explorer for the Pocket PC.

Technology	Internet Explorer for the Pocket PC
ActiveX Controls	Not supported
Auto-complete URL	Yes
Cache	Yes
Cascading Style Sheets	Not supported
Color	16K color

(continued)

(continued)

Technology	Internet Explorer for the Pocket PC
Cookies	50 elements, 4 KB max each
DHTML	Not supported
Downloading of controls	Not supported
Favorites	Yes
File formats	GIF, JPEG, BMP, XBM, HTML, and TXT
	No animated GIFs
Font downloading	Not supported
HTML	Tags defined in HTML 3.2, including tables, forms, and frames
	No floating frames
	No Virtual Reality Modeling Language (VRML)
Input devices	Touch screen, keyboard
Java	Via third parties
Link highlighting	Underlined
Protocol	HTTP 1.1 (http, https), FTP, NNTP, file://, and AvantGo
Recording file formats	WAV
Scripting	Microsoft Windows CE Jscript 3.0 (ECMA-262 compliant) No VBscript
Security	40-bit; 128-bit with add-on software download
Subscription and offline browsing	Yes
User Agent (UA) String	Mozilla 2.0/Internet Explorer 3.02
User Authentication	Basic
XML Support	Yes Data islands supported

Browsing the Internet

Browsing the Internet with Internet Explorer for the Pocket PC is similar to the desktop PC browsing experience. You don't have to take the time to learn a whole new browsing tool.

To browse the Internet, you must first make a connection to the Internet. (For information on setting up and establishing a connection, see Chapter 4.)

Once a connection is made, Internet Explorer for the Pocket PC works on top of that connection. Whether your Internet connection is a wireless connection or a phone line connection, all you have to do is open Internet Explorer for the Pocket PC, and you should be able to type a Web address and get connected to the requested Web site.

If you are making a connection in a corporate environment, you might need to access the Internet using a proxy server in order to browse the Web with the Pocket PC. As mentioned in Chapter 3, the proxy server is responsible for taking multiple Web site requests from different employees within the organization and sorting those requests to allow each a connection to the Internet through the server. I'll discuss the proxy server in the section "The Connections Tab" later in this chapter.

Changing Views

Internet Explorer for the Pocket PC has a couple of options for changing the screen layout. For example, you can use the Fit To Screen option to see more of the Web page on the Pocket PC's smaller screen. This option can reduce the size of graphics by as much as 50 percent. Enable or disable Fit To Screen under the View option of the browser window.

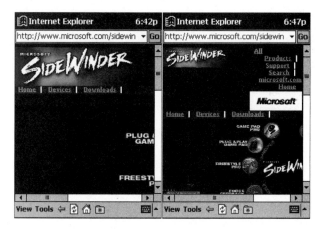

Internet Explorer for the Pocket PC also has a nice feature to reduce the amount of screen real estate taken up by the address bar. Tap the View menu at the bottom of the browser window, and then tap Address Bar to toggle between showing and hiding the address bar.

Sending a Web Link in E-Mail

In Internet Explorer for the Pocket PC, you can send someone the Web address of the page that you are visiting by going to the Tools menu and tapping Send Link Via E-Mail. Your e-mail application on the Pocket PC will open, and you will be prompted for the address of the person you want to send the link to. Before you send a link in e-mail, be sure your e-mail application is set up properly for your system. (See Chapter 9 for more information on configuring your Pocket PC to send and receive e-mail.)

Customizing Your Browsing Environment

Just like the desktop version of Internet Explorer, Internet Explorer for the Pocket PC allows you to customize your browsing environment. The Options selection, found under the Tools menu, allows you to change your home page, delete temporary Internet files, and customize your connection for a corporate environment. Changing some of these settings might allow you to browse the Internet faster than normal. There are three tabs in the Options area of Internet Explorer: General, Connections, and Advanced.

The General Tab

The General tab allows you to change the default home page of the browser.

The default home page is the Web page that you select as the page that appears when you click the home icon at the bottom of the browser window.

If you want the page that you're currently viewing in Internet Explorer for the Pocket PC to be your home page, click Use Current in the Home Page section on the General tab. Clicking Use Default will return to the Pocket PC's default home page—the page you saw when you turned it on for the first time.

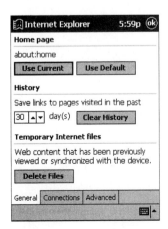

The General tab also gives you the option to clear the history. The History feature keeps track of where you have been during your Web adventures. You can see the history by tapping View in Internet Explorer and then selecting the History menu item.

The General tab also has a setting for temporary Internet files. Whenever you visit a Web site, the majority of the objects that you see are downloaded directly to the Pocket PC. This allows you to view the content of the Web page quickly as you scroll through. This is the same experience you probably have on your desktop PC version of Internet Explorer. However, just as they can on the desktop PC, temporary Internet files can take up a lot of precious storage space. Since storage space on the Pocket PC is invaluable, you should occasionally delete your temporary Internet files by tapping Delete Files. This will free storage space and will make the Pocket PC perform better overall.

The Connections Tab

The Connections tab allows you to customize the type of connection that you make to the Internet. The Pocket PC has the versatility to make different types of connections. It can make connections to the Internet in a home environment or a corporate environment. In either environment, your Web browsing experience is essentially the same. Only the connection method changes.

The type of connection that you have configured on the Pocket PC will show up in the Connection Type section. If you make a connection before you open Internet Explorer, you don't have to worry about this configuration because the connection you make will be the default type of connection. The Access Remote Content Automatically option is designed for situations in which you have not established a connection to the Internet. The selected connection is dialed every time you go to a Web site. To add other connections, select Make New Connection from the Connection Type drop-down list.

In addition to the automatic connection, there is also a setting for a proxy server. As mentioned, a proxy server is usually used in a corporate setting, where multiple people in an organization need access to the Internet. If you are using a local ISP, you won't need to configure this setting. When a proxy server is used, you must specify the server address and a port for the Pocket PC. If you want to view information on your organization's private network (intranet), you might want to check the Bypass Proxy For Local Addresses box. Since the intranet is not part of the Internet, checking this box allows for a faster browsing experience for local addresses. If you are unsure of whether you need to configure a proxy server or if you are unsure what the settings should be, consult your system administrator.

The Advanced Tab

The third tab under Options is the Advanced tab, where you'll find settings for performance and security. By default, all the items listed under this tab are selected. You might need to deselect certain items depending on your needs.

As you browse different Web sites with your Pocket PC, you might come across a Web site that requires a username and a password. Sometimes your username and password are stored on your Pocket PC as a cookie. These cookies, unlike the ones that you find in your kitchen, are small files that store information about your last connection to specific Web sites. Cookies can store information such as usernames, passwords, and zip codes. The browser uses this information the next time you go to the Web site that you received the cookie from. If you don't want Internet Explorer for the Pocket PC to accept any cookies, clear the Allow Cookies check box on the Advanced tab.

Using Favorites

So far, we have talked about connecting to the Internet and browsing with Internet Explorer for the Pocket PC. To actually connect to the Internet, you will need some sort of physical connection: a phone line, a LAN network connection (for corporate users), or a wireless connection. What if you don't have access to any of these types of connection and you need to check out stock reports or read the latest articles from MSNBC? You can use something called offline content. In Chapter 3, you learned that you could synchronize content from the desktop PC with the Pocket PC using Microsoft ActiveSync. You can also synchronize mobile favorites with your Pocket PC. The Favorites feature helps you keep track of your favorite Web sites and allows you to access them easily. It stores a customizable list of Web sites. You can make many of these Web sites available for viewing offline. That means that when you do not have a network connection, you can still view the actual Web pages in Internet Explorer. This allows for tremendous flexibility if you are using a Pocket PC and you know in advance that you will be away from an Internet connection.

Synchronizing favorites is just a matter of locating the Web sites that you want to synchronize and adding them to your Favorites list. If you want specific favorites added to your Pocket PC, you will need to add them to the Mobile Favorites folder under the Favorites menu in Internet Explorer on the desktop PC. To add a link to the Mobile Favorites folder, follow these steps:

1. On the desktop PC, use Internet Explorer to navigate to a Web site that you want to add to your Favorites list.

2. From the Favorites menu, choose Add To Favorites to open the Add Favorite dialog box.

3. Enter a name for the Web site, and select the Mobile Favorites folder as a location of storage.

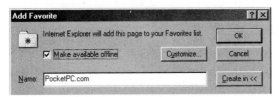

4. If you want the content of the Web site to be available on the Pocket PC when an Internet connection is not present, check the Make Available Offline check box.

5. If you select Make Available Offline, you can customize the content. Click the Customize button to start the Offline Favorite Wizard. You can use this wizard to make linked Web pages available offline, set up a synchronization schedule, and enter site-specific usernames and passwords.

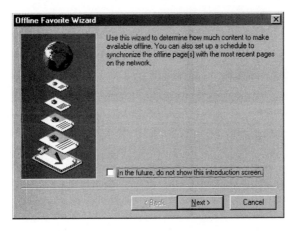

> **Note** If you choose to synchronize linked pages, be prepared for a long synchronization time. Also note that this type of synchronization consumes a large amount of memory.

6. After you select appropriate options, click OK to close the Add Favorite dialog box.

Once you have your favorite Web sites listed in the Mobile Favorites folder, you can configure ActiveSync to synchronize those Mobile Favorites. Refer to Chapter 3 for a detailed discussion of how to synchronize Mobile Favorites.

The Mobile Favorites content should appear on the Pocket PC after synchronization. As mentioned, to view the Mobile Favorites content on a Pocket PC, tap the yellow folder icon within the Internet Explorer application on the Pocket PC.

You will then see a list of Mobile Favorites in addition to AvantGo channels. A few of the favorites might be grayed, which indicates that those particular Web sites cannot be viewed offline. They might have components that require an Internet connection to be viewed.

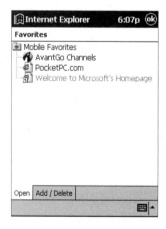

Summing Up

Internet Explorer for the Pocket PC has many of the same features that you are familiar with from the desktop version of Internet Explorer. You can browse the Web to many of your favorite Web sites, and you can view most of those Web sites online or offline. Mobile Favorites lets you synchronize many of your most important Web sites directly with the Pocket PC.

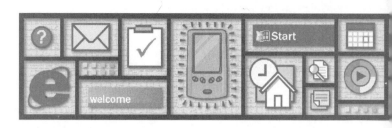

9

Using E-Mail on the Pocket PC

E-mail has become a wildly popular method of communication. If you can access the Internet, you can send and receive e-mail from just about anywhere in the world. As we become more and more mobile, using e-mail becomes an even more mainstream form of communication.

The Pocket PC can send and receive e-mail just as your desktop PC or laptop can. If you are accustomed to using your desktop PC or laptop for e-mail, you won't have too much trouble with the Pocket PC.

What Kind of E-Mail Can the Pocket PC Send and Receive?

The Pocket PC supports many industry standards. E-mail is no exception. In the Internet community, the two most popular e-mail types are Post Office Protocol version 3 (POP3) and Internet Message Access Protocol version 4 (IMAP4). Both are supported on the Pocket PC. Depending on your Internet service provider (ISP), you will need to configure your Pocket PC for one of these types. Although the technologies are different, the configuration method is similar. If you are unsure whether your ISP is POP3 or IMAP4, you might need to consult your ISP for the details. In this chapter, I'll discuss configurations for both IMAP4 and POP3.

Another popular form of e-mail that you can use on the Pocket PC is Web-based e-mail. E-mail from services such as Hotmail can be used with the browser on the Pocket PC. These services don't require special configuration. All you need to do is open Microsoft Internet Explorer for the Pocket PC and browse to the login page of the e-mail Web site. You can then use the Pocket PC to send and receive Web-based e-mail directly from the browser window.

You can also synchronize your e-mail with the Pocket PC using Microsoft ActiveSync. This method involves downloading e-mail to your device for later use. Refer to the section "Synchronize with ActiveSync" later in this chapter for a detailed discussion about how to use ActiveSync to synchronize your e-mail.

Configuring the Pocket PC for E-Mail

As I mentioned earlier, POP3 and IMAP4 are different technologies with similar configuration methods. Don't let the terms scare you. IMAP4 and POP3 simply refer to two different types of e-mail servers. The difference between an IMAP4 server and a POP3 server is in the way that your e-mail is presented. If you use a POP3 server, you can only see e-mail in the Inbox folder. You can't see other folders on your server using POP3. The IMAP4 server allows you to see all your folders and all the mail in those folders on the server. In addition, you will find that POP3 is more popular with many ISPs than IMAP4. IMAP4 is more commonly found in a corporate environment.

> **Note**   America Online (AOL) does not support POP3 or IMAP4 mail. However, if AOL is your ISP, you are not out of luck. AOL has a mail utility that you can use to receive your e-mail on the Pocket PC. Depending on the model of the Pocket PC, this AOL utility is either preinstalled on the Pocket PC or included on a supplemental CD-ROM in the box with the Pocket PC.

The IMAP4 and POP3 servers are usually owned by your ISP, and with the right login credentials, you can gain access to them and send and receive e-mail. When you receive the initial information about logging in to your ISP, you are also given a POP3 or an IMAP4 mail server name, usually in the form of *pop3.email.msn.com* or something similar.

You might be saying to yourself at this point, "I don't have the slightest clue what my e-mail server name is." You probably received a disk in the mail that had an automatic installer that installed your software and configured the e-mail on your desktop PC for you. If so, consult your ISP for the settings that you need for the Pocket PC.

The following steps will configure your Pocket PC to send and receive e-mail. This might seem like a lot of steps. However, I've included a little more detail than you would normally need when configuring your Pocket PC to send and receive e-mail. Also, keep in mind that you don't have to go through all these steps every time you want to send and receive e-mail—only the first time.

1. Tap Start, and then tap Inbox.

2. From the menu at the bottom of the Inbox screen, select Services, and then tap New Service.

3. From the Service Name window, select the service type that you need to use for your ISP—either IMAP4 or POP3.

4. You can give the service a name in the Service Name field. You can either leave the default name or create a new name. Creating a distinct name will be important when or if you configure your Pocket PC to connect to multiple e-mail accounts.

5. Tap Next to display the first setup screen.

6. Select the connection type from the drop-down list. The connection type is the connection to the ISP that the Pocket PC will use to send and receive e-mail. You should have already created these connections in Chapter 4.

7. In the Server field, enter the name of the e-mail server provided to you by your ISP. This is your POP3 or IMAP4 server, and it will be responsible for receiving your e-mail.

8. In the User ID and Password fields, enter the username and password for your e-mail account. Sometimes these are different from the username and password that you use to log in to your ISP, so check with your ISP to be sure you're using the right username and password.

9. Tap Next to display the second setup screen. The Domain field on this screen is usually used when you make a connection to a corporate server. The domain provides you with Microsoft Windows NT authentication to the e-mail system. If you are using a noncorporate ISP, you won't need to add anything to this box.

10. In the SMTP Host For Sending Mail field, enter the Simple Mail Transfer Protocol (SMTP) host that is responsible for sending your e-mail.

> **Note** Usually two servers are involved in sending and receiving your e-mail. They are typically a combination of a POP3 and an SMTP server, or an IMAP4 and an SMTP server. The POP3 and IMAP4 servers do the receiving of the e-mail, and the SMTP servers do the sending. Sometimes these are separate physical servers; at other times, they are actually the same server in one. It depends on the configuration of the e-mail system. Again, your ISP should be able to provide you with your SMTP server name.

11. In the Return Address field, enter your return address. Usually your return address is just your full e-mail address.

12. Tap Next to display the third setup screen. Several settings on this screen can be changed, but you are usually fine keeping the settings at their defaults.

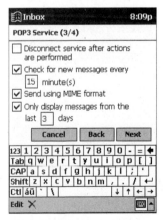

13. Tap Next to display the last setup screen. On this screen, you are presented with a choice: Get Message Headers Only or Get Full Copy Of Messages. Message headers are the first few lines of the message. Use the setting below this list box to change the number of message lines that you want to download. This option lets you limit the amount of memory e-mail takes up on the device.

If you were configuring an IMAP4 server, you would have the option Only Synchronize Inbox Folder on this screen. Checking this option will synchronize only the Inbox items, not the entire folder list. The selection Get Meeting Requests is an option that exists only with the POP3 server configuration. To fully use this feature, you will need to get full copies of your e-mail. When full copies are retrieved from the server, meeting requests will be downloaded with your e-mail.

The option Get File Attachments is available with the POP3 server settings and is useful only when you configure the setting to retrieve full copies of the message from the server. If you were configuring an IMAP4 server, you would have the option When Getting Full Copy, Get File Attachments/Meeting Requests. This option is equivalent to the combination of the two options available with the POP3 server settings. It allows you to download and store meeting requests and file attachments when getting full copies of messages.

14. Tap Finish.

Sending and Receiving Messages

Now that you have the Pocket PC configured to send and receive e-mail, let's walk through the steps of actually receiving your e-mail with your Pocket PC. You must first connect to your ISP to get an Internet connection. Once you are connected, follow these steps:

1. Tap Start, and then tap Inbox.

2. Under the Services menu at the bottom of the Inbox screen, you will see the service that you named when you configured the Pocket PC to send and receive e-mail. A black dot indicates the service you selected. If you have multiple services, you need to select the one that you want to retrieve your newest e-mail.

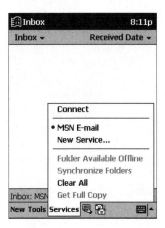

3. Once you select your service, go to the Services menu and tap Connect. If everything is configured properly, your Pocket PC should now be receiving new e-mail.

To open a message, simply tap the mail item. From this point, you can forward or reply to that message, just as with your desktop PC.

To create a new message, tap New in the lower left corner of the Inbox screen. You then need to enter the e-mail address of the person to whom you want to send the e-mail. After you've written your message, tap Send, and the message will move to the Outbox on the Pocket PC. The message is either sent directly (if you are connected to your ISP) or saved to be sent later (when you make a connection to your ISP or when you synchronize your e-mail Inbox with the desktop PC).

Sending and receiving e-mail on the Pocket PC is similar to sending and receiving e-mail on the desktop PC. The biggest difference is that you must select Connect from the Services menu on the Inbox screen when you want to receive new e-mail messages.

Mail Attachments

One of the great features of the Pocket PC is its ability to send and receive e-mail with Microsoft Word and Microsoft Excel files attached to the e-mail. This feature lets you receive an e-mail message from a colleague that contains a Word or an Excel document, open that attachment, make changes, and send it back again.

When an e-mail with an attachment arrives in your Inbox, you'll see a small paper clip icon next to the icon that represents the e-mail. When you open the e-mail message, you will see the attachment in the lower portion of the message. All you need to do is tap that icon, and the corresponding application (Word or Excel) will open and the document can be edited. If the icon is grayed and doesn't respond when you tap it, you need to download a full version of the mail message instead of just the header of the mail message. To download the full version of the e-mail with the attachments, highlight the mail message, go to the Services menu, and select Get Full Copy.

To send an attachment, open a message and tap the paper clip icon with the plus icon at the bottom of the window. You will then be able to browse the device for the file that you want to attach.

Synchronizing with ActiveSync

So far, you have seen how to send and receive e-mail directly on the Pocket PC. Not only can you send and receive e-mail from an ISP such as MSN, but you can also synchronize your e-mail from your desktop PC. As you learned in Chapter 3, you can use ActiveSync to synchronize your information, including the contents of your desktop Inbox, with the Pocket PC.

With ActiveSync, you can take your e-mail with you and have it when you need it. Let's say you have ActiveSync configured to synchronize the contents of the Inbox on your desktop PC with the Inbox on the Pocket PC. At any time, you can remove your Pocket PC from its cradle and have the same Inbox content on the Pocket PC as on your desktop PC as long as the contents of the Inbox on your desktop PC remain unchanged after the removal. This scenario is considered *offline mode:* you have access to the data that is local on the Pocket PC and not to data that is available from a server. So how do you respond to an e-mail? Since you don't have a live connection back to an e-mail server, you might feel as though you cannot reply to or forward the e-mail on your Pocket PC. However, you can. You can essentially send mail the same way you received it on the device in the first place. After you have responded to your e-mail, all you have to do is put the Pocket PC back in its docking cradle and allow it to synchronize with the desktop computer. If your desktop computer has a live connection to your e-mail server, mail that you respond to in offline mode is sent automatically. All you really have to worry about is a single setting in ActiveSync. Open the Microsoft ActiveSync window on your desktop PC; on the Tools menu, click Options; and then check Inbox in the list box. Click the Settings button to open the Inbox Synchronization Settings dialog box. Make sure the check box next to Automatically Send All Messages In The Outbox Folders Of These Selected Services is checked, and make sure there is a check in the check box next to the appropriate service that represents the connected Pocket PC.

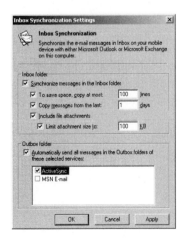

Some people use Inbox sync as the primary way to get e-mail on their Pocket PC. If this is the method you'd like to use as the primary way to get e-mail on your Pocket PC, be sure you know about the settings for synchronizing your e-mail Inbox in the Inbox Synchronization Settings dialog box.

The first setting is Synchronize Messages In The Inbox Folder. If this setting is not selected, you will not be able to synchronize your Inbox on the desktop PC with the Inbox on the Pocket PC or vice versa. The remaining settings are essentially for space-saving purposes. Remember that memory on the Pocket PC is valuable; these settings allow you to adjust the amount of information that gets synchronized with the Pocket PC. The second option, To Save Space, Copy At Most: N Lines, allows you to adjust the number of lines of a message that are downloaded to the device. Typically the default of 100 lines allows you to see most of the e-mail that you receive. The third option, Copy Messages From The Last: N Days, limits the number of days from which you download content to the Pocket PC. If you are like me and receive hundreds of e-mails each day, you won't want every single one downloaded to your Pocket PC. If you keep up with your mail, one day is usually good for synchronizing the most current information with your Pocket PC. The last option, Include File Attachments, lets you decide whether to download e-mail attachments with the mail that you synchronize. Sometimes people will send large attachments without thinking about what the recipient uses to download the e-mail. Too many e-mails with large attachments can quickly use up your memory. The default 100-KB limit works pretty well for most attachments received in e-mail.

Summing Up

E-mail is the basis of Internet communication. The Pocket PC lets you connect to a variety of e-mail services. You can connect to Web-based e-mail with Internet Explorer for the Pocket PC, and you can synchronize your e-mail with your Pocket PC from your desktop PC by using ActiveSync. You can also use industry-standard methods to send and receive e-mail to and from your ISP using POP3 and IMAP4 servers. With a wide array of e-mail solutions, the Pocket PC is the ultimate mobile e-mail machine.

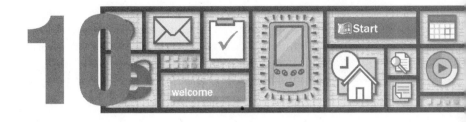

Using the Calendar

Like many Pocket PC owners, you probably purchased your Pocket PC to help make your life more organized. With so many features combined in a nice wrapper, the Pocket PC might usurp your desktop as your PC of choice. You might even discover that being organized can be fun!

So far, you've seen that the Pocket PC can be connected to your most essential information. With e-mail and Web-browsing capabilities, the Pocket PC pushes the boundaries of a normal personal digital assistant. But what about the normal functions that most PDAs have, such as managing appointments and contact lists? The Pocket PC has these features also. In this chapter, I'll discuss the Calendar application, which keeps your appointments organized.

Adding Appointments to the Calendar

The Calendar application is one of my favorite applications. I use it daily. It is simple to use and quickly tells me what I need to know. Since the Pocket PC uses Microsoft ActiveSync to synchronize automatically with the desktop PC, updating the calendar on the Pocket PC is one less thing for you to worry about.

Synchronization is one way to get new appointments into the Pocket PC. You can also enter them into the Pocket PC directly. To enter an appointment, follow these steps:

1. From the Start Menu, tap Calendar.

2. In the Calendar application, tap New in the lower left corner.

3. Enter the subject of the appointment, along with the location, times, and dates.

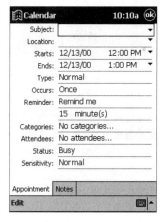

4. Tap OK in the upper right corner.

The new appointment will now appear in your appointment list on the date that you specified. To open the appointment, just tap it in the Calendar application.

Setting Reminders

When you create an appointment, you have the option of setting a reminder that will let you know in advance the appointment is coming up. For example, you might want to be reminded of your father's birthday a day ahead of time, or you might want a reminder 15 minutes before you have to be in that budget meeting. You can configure each of your reminders for different times and different durations. To set a reminder for an appointment, follow these steps:

1. In the Calendar application, tap the appointment to display the summary screen of the appointment.

2. Tap the upper portion of the summary screen to display the Properties screen of the appointment.

3. In the Reminder field, select Remind Me from the drop-down list. Selecting None from the drop-down list will disable a reminder for the appointment.

4. Tap the minutes displayed to change how many minutes before the appointment you want to be reminded.

5. Tap OK in the upper right corner.

On the same Properties screen, you can also change other properties of the appointment, such as the duration or day of the appointment. Keep in mind that if you make a change on your Pocket PC, you will need to either manually make the same change on your desktop PC or synchronize your Pocket PC back with your desktop PC.

Recurring Appointments

A recurring appointment is an appointment that occurs regularly at a specific time and date, such as a birthday or a weekly staff meeting. To make an appointment recurring, all you need to do is modify the setting for the Occurs field on the Properties screen of the appointment. This setting allows you to change an appointment to yearly or weekly. You can even edit the pattern of occurrence: Tap the Occurs field, select <Edit pattern>, and follow the wizard to customize the pattern of occurrence. You can configure your recurring appointment for specific weekly, daily, or even yearly occurrences.

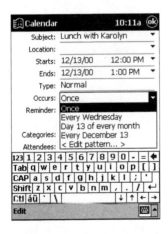

All-Day Appointments

When you're on vacation or out of the office, you might want to configure an all-day appointment on your Pocket PC. To block out an entire day, just go to the Properties screen of the appointment and change the setting for the Type field from Normal to All Day. When you change this setting to All Day, the start and end times in the Starts and Ends fields will no longer be shown.

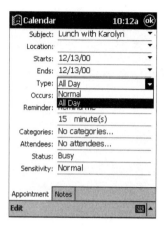

Categorizing Your Appointments

The Pocket PC has a tool that helps you organize your personal information. Let's say you use your Pocket PC primarily for business, but you also use it to keep track of some personal information. The Categories feature in the Calendar lets you categorize certain appointments as either business or personal. You can also organize your appointments according to the categories you created.

To assign a category to an appointment, follow these steps:

1. In the Calendar application, tap the appointment to display the summary screen of the appointment.

2. Tap the upper portion of the summary screen to display the Properties screen of the appointment.

3. Tap the Categories field to display a list of possible categories to choose from. The Business and Personal categories are shown by default. You can tap the Add/Delete tab at the bottom of the screen to create your own categories or remove categories that are already in the list.

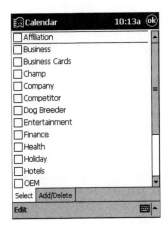

4. After you choose a category, tap OK twice in the upper right corner.

> **Note**   To modify the category of a recurring appointment, you need to open the series instead of the single occurrence.

If you are a busy person with a lot of appointments to remember, categorizing your appointments will make your life easier. To view your categorized appointments, in the Calendar application, tap View and then select Categories. You will be presented with a list of categories that you have assigned to your appointments. Select the categories that you want to see, and tap OK.

> **Note**   As I mentioned, categories enable you to select only the appointments you want to view. However, keep one thing in mind: If you forget that you have certain categories selected, you might find that you don't have an appointment or two on a given day. For example, if you forget that you have the Personal category selected, your business appointments might not be displayed when you view your categorized appointments on a particular day.

Changing the Views in the Calendar

People have different preferences when it comes to viewing items on their computer or PDA device. Fortunately, the Pocket PC can customize the views of the Calendar. All you need to do is tap View at the bottom of the Calendar screen, and you can select the view that best meets your needs. There are five different views: Agenda, Day, Week, Month, and Year. Each has a different way of representing the contents of the Calendar. You are probably familiar with the Day, Week, Month, and Year views, but what's Agenda? The Agenda view shows you all of your appointments on the selected day and the times that they occur. Unlike the Day view, the Agenda view shows you only your appointments and not the free time that you have between the appointments. You can also access the different views by pressing the hardware button on the face of your device that represents the Calendar.

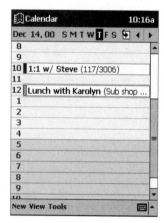

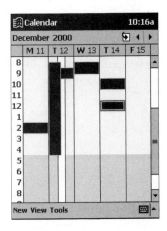

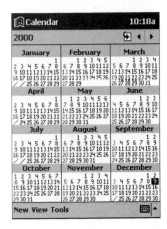

Removing Appointments

Removing appointments is simple once you know how. You will notice that there is no menu option in the Calendar application to delete appointments. To conserve space on the menus, the delete option was moved to a different location on the Pocket PC. If you see the appointment you want to delete in the Calendar, all you need to do is tap and hold that appointment to open a pop-up menu. Then select Delete Appointment from the menu.

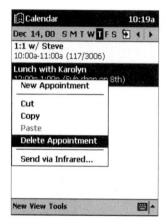

If the appointment you are deleting is a recurring appointment, a message will pop up asking whether you want to delete all appointments in the recurring series. If you choose Yes, all the appointments in the series will be deleted. If you choose No, only the appointment on that particular day will be deleted.

In addition, if you want to move an appointment to either a different time in the day or a different day altogether, all you need to do is tap and hold the appointment and select Cut from the pop-up menu. Go to the time that you want to move the appointment to, and select Paste. You can also select Copy from the pop-up menu to make a copy of the same appointment on a different day.

Summing Up

The Calendar is designed to help you be more organized and productive. If you have a lot of appointments to keep track of, you will find that the Categories feature will help you give some order to those appointments. The different calendar views demonstrate how powerful and versatile the Calendar application can be.

Using Contacts

As an on-the-go person, you want to retrieve information reliably and quickly. You might have hundreds or even thousands of contacts. If you're like most people, you probably have at least two addresses (work and home) and two or three phone numbers. Keeping track of this information can be cumbersome. The Contacts application lets the Pocket PC store a nearly limitless number of entries (restricted only by the amount of storage available) with multiple fields of information. The Contacts application contains some elegant and clever data-retrieval techniques. In addition, it offers much of the same functionality as the Calendar application, such as the ability to organize your information by category. And the tight integration between the Contacts application and Microsoft Outlook means that you don't have to re-create your contact information on the desktop PC or the Pocket PC.

Creating a Contact

Creating a contact on the Pocket PC is simple. To create a contact, follow these steps:

1. From the Start Menu, tap Contacts.
2. In the Contacts application, tap New in the lower portion of the contact list window. You are then presented with a window containing fields for entering information about the contact.

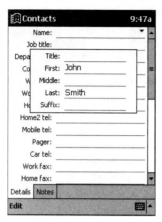

The contact entry window lets you add several entries to one main field. For example, on the Name field you will see a small black arrow pointing down. If you click that arrow, you will see subfields such as Title, First Name, Middle Name, Last Name, and Suffix.

3. After you've entered the information, tap OK in the upper right corner, and the new contact will be added alphabetically to the contact list.

Finding Contacts

If you have several hundred contacts, you might have a hard time finding a particular person. The Pocket PC has several different methods for finding a contact.

Alphabetical Sort

In the Contacts application of the Pocket PC, you will see several buttons at the top of the screen. Each button contains three characters of the alphabet. Tapping a button with your stylus will bring you to the first contact whose last name begins with that letter. For example, if you are looking for a name that starts with the letter J, all you need to do is tap the IJK button twice. Tapping the button three times will bring you to the name starting with the letter K. (Remember that the Pocket PC sorts by last name.)

Quick Scroll Sort

All Pocket PCs have a hardware button for scrolling. This button is usually located on the side or the front of the device. If you keep this button scrolling forward or backward, a white box containing letters of the alphabet appears on the screen. When you see the first letter of the name you are looking for, just release the scroll button. That area of the alphabet will be shown in the list.

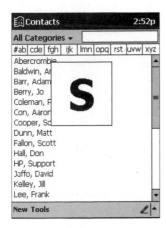

Name Entry Sort

Another quick way to find a contact is to type in the person's name. In the upper right corner of the Contacts application, you will see a box where you can enter information. Let's say that you want to find a contact with the last name Johnston. Start typing the word *John*, and all your entries containing John in either the last name or the first name will appear. You can use the keyboard, the character recognizer, or the transcriber for entering the name. This sort method is especially convenient when you aren't quite sure of the name or its complete spelling. For example, you might remember that the name has John in it, but you aren't sure whether John is in the first name or the last name. This method presents you with any name that contains the word John.

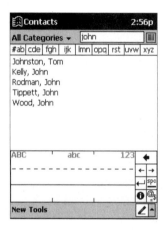

Categorizing Contacts

Throughout this book, you have seen many different ways that the Pocket PC can help keep you organized. One way is with categories. When you have hundreds or even thousands of contacts in your Pocket PC, it's important to organize them in a way that allows you to retrieve the information quickly. By sorting your contacts into categories, you can organize your contacts any way that you like them to be organized. By default, you can choose to categorize your contacts as either business or personal. You can also create your own categories. For example, you can organize all your contacts from a particular company into a category. When you select that category from the category list, only the contacts who work for that company will appear. Keep in mind that whether you choose to use default categories or make your own, categories will always get synchronized with Outlook on the desktop PC.

To categorize your contacts, all you need to do is assign a category to a contact at the time you create the contact. You can also change the category of an existing contact by following these steps:

1. Open a contact in the Contacts application.

2. Tap the name of the contact to display the window containing information about the contact.

3. Tap the Categories field, and you will see a list of possible categories to choose from. You will also see the Add/Delete tab at the bottom of the screen. This lets you create your own categories or remove categories that are in the list already.

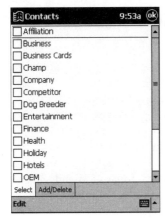

4. After you choose a category, tap OK twice in the upper right corner.

Now that you have your categories assigned, let's look at how to view contacts associated with those categories. In the upper left corner of the Contacts application, you will see a category drop-down menu. By default, it will say All Categories. When you tap All Categories, you will see the categories that you use most often. Select the category that you want to see, and the contact list will re-sort and show you the contacts listed by that category.

In addition to selecting the desired category from the drop-down list in the upper left corner of the Contacts application, you can also use the hardware button on the face of your Pocket PC that represents contacts to switch between categories that you use on a regular basis. When you press the button, you are taken through the different categories that you are using for your contacts. Each category is shown along with the contacts associated with those categories. As you continue to press the contacts hardware button, you will eventually return to the default selection, All Categories.

> **Note** Categories can be tricky. If you forget that you have certain categories selected, it might look as if several of your contacts are missing. In reality, you're seeing only what's listed under the category you've selected.

Sending a Contact to Another Pocket PC

Can you imagine a day when you will no longer hand your business card to a new business contact? That day is just around the corner. Infrared communication lets you beam an electronic business card to future business prospects. In your contact list, you might have a contact entry for yourself that contains all the necessary information for a person to contact you. All you need to do to send that contact entry to another Pocket PC user is tap and hold the contact in the list and select Send Via Infrared. The receiving Pocket PC will need to be set up to receive the contact. To do this, tap Tools in the Contacts application and select Receive Via Infrared. Then align the two devices, and the information will be passed between them.

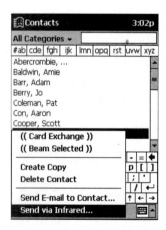

Note   If you want to send a contact to a Palm or Handspring user, you will need to install additional third-party software.

Synchronizing Contacts

Just as you did with your appointments, you can use Microsoft ActiveSync to synchronize the contacts on your desktop PC with those on your Pocket PC. When you first install ActiveSync, the synchronizing contacts option is selected by default. To change the synchronization setting of contacts, open ActiveSync on your desktop PC and select Tools from the menu, and then select Options. From the list, highlight Contacts and click Settings. You can choose to synchronize all contacts or a specific few. You can also choose to synchronize contacts from specific categories. However, before you can see entries in this window, you must fully synchronize at least one time. Once this initial synchronization is complete, you can modify the settings for your needs. Refer to Chapter 3 for a detailed discussion on how to conduct the initial synchronization.

Removing Contacts

Sometimes you might need to remove a contact from your contact list. To delete a contact, tap and hold the contact that you want to delete in the contacts list. Then select Delete Contact from the menu.

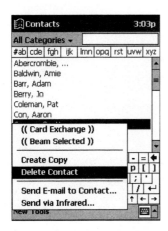

A confirmation dialog box will appear, asking you whether to continue with the deletion of the contact. By choosing Yes, you will delete the contact. Choosing No takes you back to the contact list without deleting the contact.

Summing Up

The Pocket PC brings together the basics of contact management. With several different methods of searching through your contacts, the Pocket PC gives you the flexibility to manage hundreds or even thousands of contacts. You can use categories to customize how you view your contacts information. We've come a long way from the "little black book." Now we can be digitally organized with the Pocket PC.

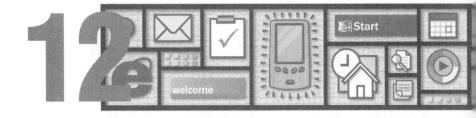

Using Tasks

The Tasks application is one of the tools that help keep you organized. You can think of it as a digital to-do list. In the past few chapters, you've learned how the tools of the Pocket PC can help you be more organized. Tasks is another application that you can use to help keep both your personal and your business environment more organized.

Task vs. Appointment

You might be wondering when you would use a task instead of an appointment. These two applications are similar, but they aren't identical. Typically you create a task when you need to remind yourself of something brief, such as items on a grocery list or maybe a TV show that you want to watch.

You'll typically use an appointment when you know ahead of time that you have something to do or a place to be. Appointments offer more options, such as start times, end times, and attendees. Unlike tasks, appointments also show up in Microsoft Outlook, indicating to others that you are busy at a certain time. If you do any group scheduling with Outlook, you will want to show your busy times using appointments instead of tasks.

Creating a Task

Creating a task is similar to creating an appointment or a contact. To create a task, follow these steps:

1. From the Start Menu, tap Tasks.

2. In the Tasks application, tap New in the lower left corner of the screen. You will be presented with a window to enter information about the task.

3. Enter the appropriate information in the information fields provided. You can enter the subject of the task, when the task starts, and when the task is due. Just as with an appointment, you can set a reminder to notify you of your task.

> **Note** The subject that you assign to the task becomes the name of the task in the task list. Therefore, it is important to give the task a name that you can identify later in the task list.

4. After you've entered the information, tap OK in the upper right corner.

In addition to creating a task by tapping New in the lower left corner, you can also create a task by entering the task name in the entry bar at the top of the task list. If the entry bar is not visible, select the Tools menu from the Tasks application and then select Entry Bar. The entry bar also enables you to set a priority of High (indicated by a red exclamation point) or Low (indicated by a blue arrow pointing down). When you create a new task by entering the subject in the entry bar, no other fields in the task, such as start times and due dates, are filled out. This is a quick way to enter a task.

Entry Bar

Categorizing Tasks

As with the Calendar and Contacts applications, you can categorize your task information for easier organization.

To categorize your tasks, all you need to do is assign a category to a task at the time you create the task. You can also change the category of an existing task by following these steps:

1. Open a task in the Tasks application.

2. Tap the name of the task to display the window containing information about the task.

3. Tap the Categories field, and you will see a list of possible categories to choose from. You will also see the Add/Delete tab at the bottom of the screen. This lets you create your own categories or remove categories that are in the list already.

4. After you choose a category, tap OK twice in the upper right corner.

In the upper left corner is the category drop-down menu that you can use to list your categories. You can choose to view individual categories established per task; you can also choose to show all active tasks and all completed tasks.

A task that is not completed is considered an active task. Most active tasks will appear black in the task list. If a task is not checked as completed by its due date, it will turn red. This feature can show you at a glance how much you're getting done, but it can also definitely show you how disorganized you are.

The hardware button on the face of your Pocket PC that represents tasks enables you to switch between categories too. When you press the button, you can see each category and the contacts associated with that category. As you continue to press the contacts hardware button, you will eventually return to the default selection, All Categories.

> **Note** If you open the Tasks application and find that many of your tasks are not listed, be sure your category selection in the upper left corner is set to All Categories. This setting allows you to see all your tasks, including ones associated with a category.

Sorting Your Tasks

You can use the sorting feature to display the tasks differently. In the upper right corner of the Tasks application, you will see a drop-down window for the Sort By feature. By tapping the small black down arrow, you can choose to sort your information by status, priority, subject, start date, or due date.

Completing and Deleting a Task

What do you do when a task is completed? For those of you out there who actually complete your tasks, all you have to do is place a check mark next to the completed task. The next time you synchronize the Pocket PC with your desktop PC, that task will show up in Outlook as completed. It will remain on the Pocket PC until it is deleted. You can delete a task by tapping and holding the task and selecting Delete from the tap-and-hold menu. A confirmation dialog box will appear, asking you whether you want to continue with the deletion of the task. By choosing Yes, you will delete the task. Choosing No takes you back to the task list without deleting the task.

Synchronizing Tasks

With Microsoft ActiveSync, you can synchronize your tasks the same way you can with the other PIM applications. In fact, many of the task settings are the same as the calendar settings.

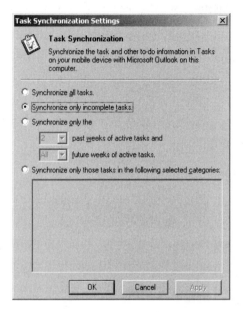

You can synchronize all tasks, only incomplete tasks, tasks of a certain time period, and tasks from specific categories. The most frequently used setting is usually the setting for synchronizing only incomplete tasks. This setting helps you avoid filling up your device or desktop PC with tasks that you've already completed.

Summing Up

Depending on how you choose to organize, the Tasks application can provide the simplest forms of figuring out what you have done and what you still need to do. And with the ability to synchronize your tasks with the desktop PC via Outlook, you can always know what tasks you need to complete and when you need to get them done.

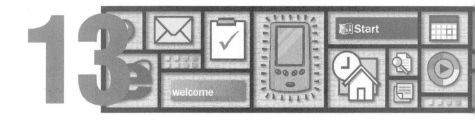

Using Notes

I'm sure you've been in a situation in which you needed to write something down quickly but you couldn't find a piece of paper and a pen. You probably ended up not writing down the information, or maybe you wrote a few notes on your hand or a napkin.

The Pocket PC will help you avoid these situations. A built-in application called Notes lets you take a quick note without frantically searching for pen and paper. Although people have been taking notes on personal digital assistants (PDAs) for years, the Pocket PC extends this functionality by letting you synchronize those notes so you have the same information on your Pocket PC and desktop PC. The Pocket PC also lets you take notes in your own handwriting as well as attach a voice note to a handwritten note.

Taking Notes

One of the nicest things about the Notes application is the variety of ways it allows you to take notes: in typed form, in handwritten form, and even by using the recording feature.

Think of the Notes application as a stack of sticky notes. You can take quick notes without having to worry about saving them. You just create a new note, write or type in your information, and close the note and it is saved. It's that simple.

To create a Note on the Pocket PC, follow these steps:

1. Tap the Start menu in the upper left corner, and select Notes. (If you are on the Today screen, you can simply tap New at the bottom of the screen and select Note from the list.)

2. The Note screen looks like a piece of notebook paper. Enter information by selecting the type of input from the lower right corner. You can select the keyboard, the Character Recognizer, or the Transcriber. You can use any of these input methods to create your note with typed text.

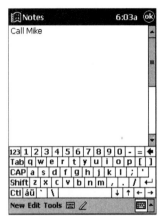

3. If you want to freehand a note without translation to text, select the pencil icon at the bottom of the screen. When you select the icon, it will have a box around it. You will also see light blue horizontal lines (a little like the lines on notebook paper) on the screen where you enter your information. When you create a new note, this input method is selected by default. You can use this method to draw shapes as well as text.

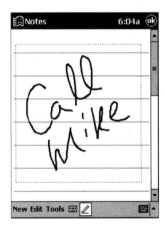

4. To attach a voice recording to the note, tap the small cassette icon at the bottom of the screen. A small window appears, containing audio controls similar to those you would find on any audio playback device. To attach a voice memo to a note, tap the red Record button. (You can also press the Record hardware button on the Pocket PC.) When your voice message is complete, tap the square button at the bottom of the window. Your voice message is now attached to the message and will appear in the form of a yellow speaker icon. To play the voice message, tap this icon. You can attach multiple voice messages.

Note Remember that audio can consume a lot of memory. Try to keep audio messages to a minimum. Also keep in mind that when you attach multiple audio messages to a note, they will be hard to keep organized because the audio icons all look alike. You might want to enter a little text next to each one to keep them organized.

5. Once the note is complete, tap OK in the upper right corner of the screen.

Sorting and Moving Notes

The notes in the note list on the Pocket PC are sorted in alphabetical order. Once you've created a note, it is added to the note list. The name of the note in the list is pulled from the actual text in the note. For example, if you create a typed text note that starts with the words *Take the dogs to the park after work*, the note will be listed as *Take the dogs to.* Typed text notes are always listed by the first few characters of the note. If you create a freehand note using the pencil tool, the note will have a generic name such as *Note1* or *Note2*.

Next to each note in the note list, you will see the size of the note. Most Pocket PCs have 32 megabytes to run applications and store your information. (One megabyte equals 1024 kilobytes, and 1 kilobyte equals 1024 bytes.) If your notes get too large for the available memory on the device, you can choose to move your notes to a storage card. To move your note, follow these steps:

1. Insert a storage card into the Pocket PC.

2. In the Notes application, tap and hold the note you want to move.

3. From the pop-up menu, select Rename/Move to display the Rename/Move window.

4. From the Location list box of the Rename/Move window, select Storage Card. (If you want to rename the note, enter the new name in the Name field of this window.)

5. Tap OK in the upper right corner.

You can also send a note to another Pocket PC by tapping and holding the item in the note list and then selecting Send Via Infrared from the pop-up menu. If you have Internet connectivity, you can also select Send Via E-Mail.

Removing a Note

Removing a note is just as easy as creating it. To remove a note, follow these steps:

1. In the list of notes on the Pocket PC, tap and hold the note you want to delete.

2. From the pop-up menu, select Delete.

3. A message will appear, asking you to confirm the deletion of the note. Tap Yes to confirm the deletion. Tapping No cancels the deletion.

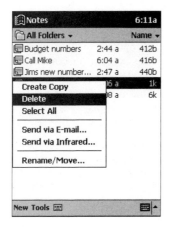

Synchronizing Notes

You can use Microsoft ActiveSync to synchronize notes on the Pocket PC with those on your desktop PC. You need to make sure the synchronizing notes option is selected in ActiveSync's Options window. You can get to this window by clicking the Tools menu in ActiveSync and then selecting Options. After you make sure there is a check mark next to Notes, click OK, and the notes on the Pocket PC will be synchronized with the desktop PC and vice versa.

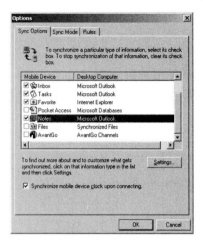

Summing Up

The Notes application on the Pocket PC is a great application for capturing quick snippets of information. Synchronization ensures that you have the same notes on your desktop PC and on your Pocket PC. The flexibility of different text conversion tools, the ability to record audio messages, and the ability to draw and take notes freehand make the Notes application a necessity that you will use often.

Microsoft Pocket Word

The Pocket PC is not a replacement for the desktop PC or the laptop. It is a complement to them. The Pocket PC provides mobile flexibility and the essential tools for completing your tasks no matter where you are. This chapter will examine the basics of Microsoft Pocket Word. Because Pocket Word is similar to the desktop version of Microsoft Word, I will discuss only the features unique to Pocket Word, rather than detailing all of its features.

Just like its cousin on the desktop PC, Pocket Word offers easy-to-use word processing power. Pocket Word is not a full-blown version of Word. Pocket Word was designed mainly to edit Word attachments that you receive in e-mail. In other words, Pocket Word acts as the application that can open and view the contents of an attachment. You can make the necessary changes to the document and then either return the mail to the sender or send the mail to the next recipient. (See Chapter 9 for more information about attachments in e-mail.)

With several methods of text input, Pocket Word lets you create documents fairly quickly. Some Pocket PCs allow a portable keyboard to be attached for faster and more comfortable text input. The ability to synchronize your information allows you to create documents on either your Pocket PC or your desktop PC and have the same content in both places.

Creating a Document

There are several ways to create a document in Pocket Word. One way is to tap Start and then tap Pocket Word. If you are opening Pocket Word for the first time, it will automatically open to a new document. You can immediately start typing.

If you've already used Pocket Word on your Pocket PC, you'll be presented with a file list of existing Pocket Word documents. You can either open an existing document by tapping it or create a new document by tapping New in the lower left corner of the screen.

Another way to create a new Pocket Word document is from the Today screen. In the lower left corner of the Today screen, tap New and then select Word Document from the pop-up menu. This will automatically take you into Pocket Word and open a new document.

Entering Information

Like most other applications on the Pocket PC, Pocket Word offers several methods of entering information: you can use the soft keyboard, the Character Recognizer, or the Transcriber. You can change the input method by tapping the input selector in the lower right corner of the screen and selecting a new input method.

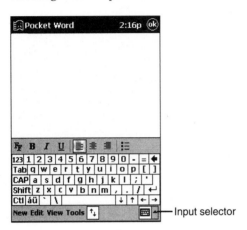 — Input selector

> **Note** If you want to create a long document, you can also enter information by using a small portable keyboard that attaches to your Pocket PC. Typically you just install the appropriate software for the keyboard and attach it to the Pocket PC. Once the keyboard is attached, the Pocket PC detects that it is present, and you are ready to start typing.

Another method of entering information is with an audio message. As you learned in the previous chapter, you can attach a voice message to a document. To attach an audio message to a document, follow these steps:

1. Position the cursor where you want the audio message to appear.

2. Press the Record hardware button on the device to record a message. The Record/Playback toolbar appears at the bottom of the screen, indicating that the recording is taking place.

3. When you hear the beep, start your recording.

4. To stop recording, either tap the Stop button on the screen or release the Record hardware button.

Using a Template

Sometimes you might find it easier to start a new document by basing it on an example. Those examples are usually called *templates*. Every Pocket PC has a templates folder containing sample documents that you can open and modify to suit your needs. Pocket Word doesn't have as many templates as the desktop version of Word has, but it has enough to get you started. You'll find templates for creating a blank document, meeting notes, a memo, a phone memo, and a to-do list in the Templates folder. Just tap the template you want to modify, and that item will open. You can also create your own templates by creating a new document and saving it to the Templates folder. This is a useful feature if you use the same document layout and style over and over.

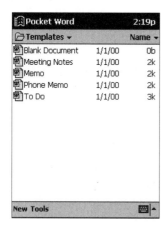

Saving Your Document

Saving a document in Pocket Word is a little different from saving a document in the desktop version of Word. When you are finished creating or modifying your document, all you need to do to save it is tap OK in the upper right corner. You will then see the document in the file list. To modify the document name or change its location, just tap and hold the file and select Rename/Move from the pop-up menu. You can then make the necessary changes to the fields provided. You can also make changes to the document name and storage location by opening the document and selecting Save Document As from the Tools menu. To save a document with the default name and location, tap OK in the upper right corner of the screen.

> **Note**   Since Pocket Word doesn't have a Save command, all modifications are saved when you tap OK in the upper right corner. There is no Cancel button. If you make a change to a document, that change will remain until you tap OK. If you don't want the change saved to the document, you need to remove the change manually before you tap OK. You can also tap New at the bottom of the window, and a message will appear, asking you to save the document first. Choose Yes, No, Cancel, or Save As. If you choose No, your changes will be lost. If you choose Save As, you can save the document under a new name.

Setting Options

In the Pocket Word application, there is a menu at the bottom of the screen called *Tools*. In the Tools menu, you'll find the Options selection, which provides a few settings you might find helpful for optimizing the Pocket Word application for your needs.

The Default Template setting lets you choose a document style as your default for creating new documents. You can choose from Blank Document, Meeting Notes, Memo, Phone Memo, and To Do.

The Save To setting lets you choose one of two default locations to store your documents: Main Memory or Storage Card. If you choose Storage Card, the documents will be stored on the storage card under the My Documents folder.

Last, the Display In List View setting lets you choose what is displayed in the file list of the Pocket Word application. The default setting is Known Types. This setting shows all known types of files that Pocket Word can open. You can also choose to show .txt and Pocket Word files or only Pocket Word files.

Cut, Copy, and Paste

To cut or copy text, simply highlight the text in the document by dragging your stylus over the text that you want to copy or cut. From the Edit menu, select Cut or Copy. Then tap the location where you want the text to appear, and select Paste from the Edit menu.

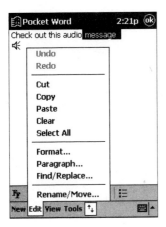

You can also cut or copy text by selecting the text you want to copy or cut, tapping and holding the highlighted text, and then selecting Cut or Copy from the pop-up menu. To paste the text, tap and hold the location where you want the text to appear and then select Paste from the pop-up menu. The text that you highlighted earlier will be placed in the chosen location.

You can also use the soft keyboard for copying and moving text, using the same commands on the Pocket PC that you use on the desktop PC. To cut text using the keyboard, highlight the text that you want to cut and then tap Ctrl-X on the keyboard. If you want to copy text, highlight the text you want to copy and then tap Ctrl-C on the keyboard. To paste the text that you either copied or cut, tap the location where you want to place the text and then tap Ctrl-V on the keyboard.

Note   The keyboard methods for cut, copy, and paste are not unique to Pocket Word. You can use these commands in any application on the Pocket PC.

Working in Different Modes

So far, you've seen how to enter information in your Pocket Word documents by using different input methods such as the Transcriber and the keyboard. You can also enter information by using different modes of Pocket Word. At the bottom of the document window, tap the View menu to see the different modes for entering information: Writing, Drawing, Typing, and Recording. The black dot next to any one of these items indicates the mode that is selected. When you select a mode, the menus change to reflect the mode that you are in. No matter what modifications you make in the different modes—even audio recordings or drawings—they will be saved as Pocket Word documents that you can synchronize with your desktop PC or send to others in e-mail.

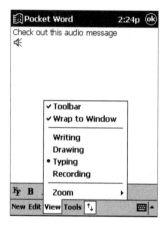

The default mode is Typing. If you select the Drawing mode, you can draw on your Pocket Word document right on top of text that is already there. Writing mode enables you to write with the stylus on the screen in a Pocket Word application. Then you can use the handwriting recognition feature contained in Pocket Word to recognize your handwriting. To use this feature, follow these steps:

1. Change the mode to Writing mode by tapping View and selecting Writing.

2. Using the stylus, write something on the screen in your own handwriting.

3. Deselect the pencil tool in the lower left corner of the screen, and highlight the handwriting you just wrote.

4. Select Recognize from the Tools menu at the bottom of the screen. The Pocket PC will translate the handwriting to regular text.

Sometimes the translation is right on, and sometimes it misses the target. If you want to use this feature, you might need to work on making your handwriting easier to read. For a detailed discussion about how to enter information in Recording mode, see Chapter 13.

Formatting Your Document

Although Pocket Word is not a complete version of Word, it contains many of the same formatting tools that you would find in the desktop PC version of Word. Changing fonts and adding bold, italics, or underlines are just a tap away. You can use the formatting menu, which appears at the bottom of the window, directly above the main Pocket Word menu. This menu varies with the mode you are in. For example, Typing mode has a different formatting menu than Drawing mode. You can hide the menu by tapping the double-arrow icon at the bottom of the screen.

In addition to using the formatting menu, you can make formatting changes to your document by selecting Format from the Edit menu at the bottom of the screen. Tapping Format displays the Format screen, which lets you change the font, style, and size of your text. You can also modify the line width and color of the drawing tool from this screen.

Documents in E-Mail

As I mentioned, Pocket Word was designed mainly for editing Word attachments that you receive in e-mail. After creating or editing a Pocket Word document on the Pocket PC, you can send it as an e-mail attachment. To send this document, simply tap and hold the filename in the file list of Pocket Word documents and select Send Via E-Mail from the pop-up menu. This will open the Inbox application and also open a new mail message with the file attached.

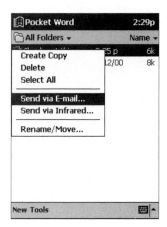

Sending a Document Through Infrared

You can also use infrared to send a Pocket Word document to another Pocket PC user. From the file list of Pocket Word documents, locate the file that you want to send. Tap and hold that document, and select Send Via Infrared from the pop-up menu. Then align the infrared port on your Pocket PC with the infrared port of the Pocket PC you want to send the document to. The two devices will begin the process of transferring the file. When the process is complete, both devices will chime and a notice of completion will appear on screen. If you are receiving a file from another Pocket PC, the file will appear on your device in the My Documents folder. You can then move it to the desired location.

Summing Up

Pocket Word is a simple text editor with minimal features. Its primary purpose is to provide enough functionality to open Word attachments in e-mail and allow you to edit them and send them back with the new edits intact. Pocket Word contains familiar Word features such as templates and formatting menus. With its different input methods, Pocket Word can become one of your favorite editing tools.

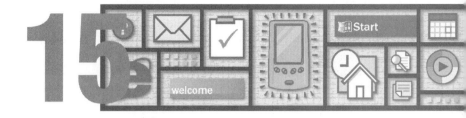

Microsoft Pocket Excel

Spreadsheets are powerful tools. From balancing your checkbook to tracking your favorite stocks, you've probably used a spreadsheet for almost every type of calculation possible. Just as Microsoft Word is widely known as the word processor of choice, Microsoft Excel is identified also as the number cruncher of choice.

In the last chapter, I discussed the basics of word processing with Microsoft Pocket Word. Like Pocket Word, Microsoft Pocket Excel is not the complete version of Excel found on the desktop PC. Despite the lack of some of the more elaborate features of Excel, however, Pocket Excel provides more than enough features and functions to assist with your mobile calculations. Since Pocket Excel works much the same as the version of Excel on your desktop, in this chapter I will focus on the basics of Pocket Excel and how it is used on the Pocket PC, and not on basic spreadsheet usage.

Creating a Document

Pocket Excel provides several ways to create a document. One way is to tap Start and then tap Pocket Excel. If this is your first time using Pocket Excel, a new document will open automatically. If you've already used Pocket Excel on your Pocket PC, the Pocket Excel application will display a file list of Pocket Excel documents stored on the Pocket PC.

Another way to create a Pocket Excel document is from the Today screen. At the bottom of the Today screen, select Excel Workbook from the New menu. This will open a new Pocket Excel document.

You can enter information by using one of the three methods that Pocket Excel offers: the Character Recognizer, the soft keyboard, or the Transcriber.

Formatting Your Document

As you probably know from using Excel on the desktop PC, Excel has many tools for formatting your document and the individual cells within that document. Pocket Excel provides many of those same tools. You'll find the majority of the formatting tools in the Format menu at the bottom of the screen in the Pocket Excel application. Use this menu to adjust the cell formats and add or remove sheets to or from your document.

Formatting Cells

Changing cell formats will probably be the formatting option you use most often. To edit the cell formats, in the Pocket Excel application, tap the Format menu at the bottom of the screen and select Cells from the menu. From here you will see tabs at the bottom of the menu. Each tab provides different options for the various types of cell formats. The Size tab is the default.

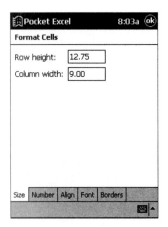

When you modify the setting on the Size tab and verify it by tapping OK in the upper right corner, the selected row height or column width will be changed. If you select several columns or rows and then change this setting, all the selected columns and rows will be modified.

The Number tab allows you to customize your data to the proper decimal locations or possibly even the best time format.

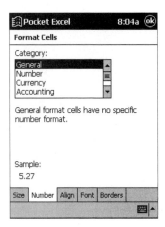

Under the Category selection at the top of the Number tab, you have different types of numbers to choose from. As you select different categories, the contents displayed in the lower portion of the Format Cell screen keep changing, providing even more items to choose from. When you have chosen the appropriate number format for your cell, tapping OK in the upper right corner will change either an individual cell or a selection of cells.

> **Note**   If you can't find the appropriate formatting option from the category list, select Custom from the list. From the lower portion of the screen, you can choose the number format that suits your needs.

Sometimes you need to align the data that you enter into your cell. For example, you might have finished entering a long list of numbers. By default, the numbers align to the right inside the cell; however, you want to align them in the center of the cell. You can change that setting on the Align tab.

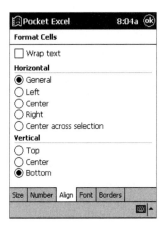

The Align tab allows you to change not only the horizontal alignment but also the vertical alignment. In addition, the Align tab has a setting that allows you to wrap text. This lets you write a long string of text in a cell without that text appearing cut off. However, the text will wrap only to the size of the cell. If the top-to-bottom size of the cell is too small, the text will appear cut off. If you use this feature, you might need to extend the size of the cell from the Size tab.

The last two tabs in the Format Cells menu are Font and Borders. These tabs can help you customize the look of your data in a spreadsheet. If you need to change the font in a cell or a series of cells, the Font tab provides the necessary options for font, size, and color. The Borders tab allows you to create borders around your data in individual cells or a series of cells. You can also change the color of the border and add a fill color to your cell.

Formatting Rows and Columns

Like the desktop version of Excel, Pocket Excel lets you hide or unhide a column or a row. To hide a column or a row, select either the column or the row, tap Format, and then select Hide from the submenu. Keep track of your use of this tool. It can be frustrating to forget that you have hidden a column or a row of data.

The Autofit option—found in the Column or the Row submenu under the Format menu—sizes the column or row according to the data within the cells. For example, let's say you have a column that mostly contains numbers that are four digits in length but also contains some cells of data with six-digit numbers. If you select Autofit from the Column submenu, the column will resize itself to the width of six digits. If at a later time you enter information that exceeds the six-digit width, the column will resize itself to the new digits.

> **Note**   If you turn on Autofit and you want the cell size to go back to a standard fixed size, you need to select Cells from the Format menu. On the Size tab, change either the row height or the column width to a number that exceeds the current values by at least one.

Modifying Sheets

Sometimes you need to break your Pocket Excel project into several pieces. Just as you do with the desktop PC version of Excel, you can use various sheets to help you organize your information. By default, every new Pocket Excel file that you open contains three sheets labeled Sheet 1, Sheet 2, and Sheet 3. To view different sheets, tap the Sheet drop-down list at the bottom of your workspace. From the drop-down list, select the sheet where you want to place or observe information.

To add more sheets to the drop-down list, select Modify Sheets from the Format menu to display the Modify Sheets screen. From there you can add or remove various sheets to or from your document. Although there is no limit to the number of sheets that you can add, the Pocket PC can display only eight sheets in the drop-down list.

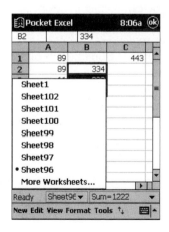

The More Worksheets option in that list, however, allows you to view more worksheets. Tapping the More Worksheets option will also take you to the Modify Sheets screen. You can use the Move Up and Move Down buttons in this screen to rearrange your sheets and place your most frequently used sheets within the top eight positions of the list. You can also rename the sheets by tapping the Rename button on this screen and providing a new name for the sheet.

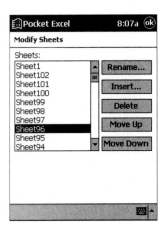

Deleting and Inserting Cells

You have several methods of removing data from your spreadsheet. You can use Cut from the Edit menu, or you can highlight the specific information you want to delete and then tap the Delete key on the soft keyboard. These methods work fine, but sometimes you need to delete a whole column or a whole row. To do this, highlight the column or the row that you want to remove. Select the Format menu, and then select Delete Cells. If you highlight several cells in a row or in a column, selecting the Format menu and then selecting Delete Cells will open the Delete Cells window. From this window, you can choose to delete an entire row or column or just move the cells up or to the left.

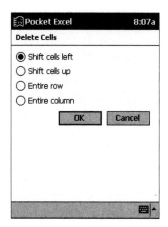

Inserting cells into a worksheet is similar to deleting cells. To insert a row or a column, highlight the cell or cells where you want to place new empty cells. From the Format menu, tap Insert Cells. From the Insert Cells window that appears, you can choose to shift cells right or down, or to insert an entire row or column.

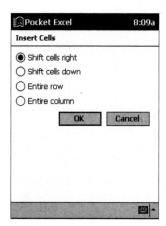

Tools

A spreadsheet is more than just an application that displays information in a nice list. Each spreadsheet contains a set of tools to manipulate your data. You can find these tools under the Tools menu in the Pocket Excel application. From there you can turn on the AutoFilter, sort your information, insert a function or a symbol, or send a Pocket Excel document in e-mail or via infrared.

Like most spreadsheet applications, Pocket Excel contains more than 100 built-in functions that allow you to do specialized calculations with your data. The functions are located in the Insert Function selection on the Tools menu.

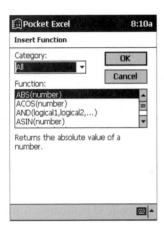

You can select the function from the Category drop-down list and then select the specific function from the Function drop-down list. You can also choose All from the Category list and then select the desired function from the Function list. Notice that most functions use placeholders as their arguments.

Once you've selected the function that you need, tap OK, and the function will be inserted into the command bar at the top of your document. To use this function, replace the placeholders in the function with the actual numbers and tap Enter on the keyboard or tap the check mark in the command bar. The result will then be placed in the highlighted cell. You don't always have to go to the Tools menu to insert a function. You can also insert the function by typing the name and format of the function in the command bar. For example, if I want to take the average of four different numbers, all I need to type in the command bar is =AVERAGE(1,2,3,4). The result is 2.5. This method will save you time if you use the same functions repeatedly.

On occasion you might need to insert specialized symbols such as © and ® into your spreadsheet. Pocket Excel contains an insert-symbol tool that lets you insert symbols not found on a keyboard. To insert a special symbol, select Insert Symbol from the Tools menu in the Pocket Excel application. Select the symbol from the list, and tap Insert. The symbol is then placed in the command bar.

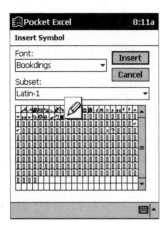

After you enter data into the spreadsheet, you might want to manipulate the way it is sorted. If you create long lists of information, you might have trouble finding specific records. Pocket Excel contains a sort feature that allows you to sort on three different columns of either ascending or descending order. This feature is located in the Sort selection on the Tools menu.

Document Passwords

Because the Pocket PC is such a small, mobile device, it can, unfortunately, be an easy target for theft. Sometimes the stolen data is worth a lot more than the device itself. Fortunately the Pocket PC has a couple of measures to help you protect the contents of your device if it ends up in the wrong hands. You can set a password to access your device. Every time the device is powered on, a password window appears, asking you to enter your four-digit password. You can obtain that device password configuration from the Settings menu under the Start menu. However, Pocket Excel also contains a password function that allows you to assign a password to one or more specific documents. To set a document password, follow these steps:

1. Open a Pocket Excel document.

2. Select Password from the Edit menu. The Password screen appears.

3. Enter your password. Your password can be text, a number, or a combination of both. Passwords are case-sensitive. For example, if you choose the password Dog3, the passwords DOG3 and dog3 won't work.

> **Note**   Try to create passwords that are hard for others to guess but easy for you to remember. If you forget your password, you will have no way to open that document.

---

4. Enter your password again to verify it. (To remove a password from a document, just make the password field blank.)

5. Tap OK. The next time you want to open this document, you need to specify the password for the document first.

Viewing Your Document

Pocket Excel includes some tools to help you view your documents better on the Pocket PC's smaller screen. From the View menu at the bottom of the screen, you have the option of turning off or on various bars. If you turn off the scroll bars, you can use the hardware scroll buttons to move up and down on the screen.

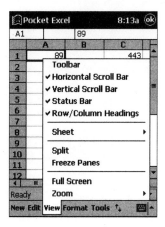

Just as you can on the desktop version of Excel, you can split and freeze panes by selecting Split or Freeze Panes from the View menu. You can deselect these settings by selecting Remove Split or Unfreeze Panes from the View menu.

Even though the Pocket PC screen is fairly large compared with that of many other personal digital assistants (PDAs) on the market, the data can still be too small to see. Pocket Excel offers a zoom tool that allows you to see the text in greater detail. To change the zoom settings, select Zoom from the View menu. From there you can select from five different preset zoom settings. You can also specify a different zoom setting from the preset settings by selecting Custom from the Zoom submenu.

Summing Up

Pocket Excel is a powerful spreadsheet application. With much of the same functionality as the desktop version of Excel, Pocket Excel provides many formatting and calculation tools. You can send Pocket Excel documents in e-mail or to another Pocket PC via infrared.

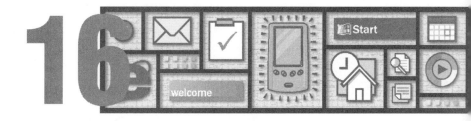

Microsoft Windows Media Player

Remember when the Sony Walkman was the talk of the town back in the 1980s? Everybody had to have one. (I know I did!) Then the rage was portable CD players. The musical fad of the new millennium seems to be digital music players. The Pocket PC is also a digital music player. What makes a digital music player so useful is that you can use the same medium to both transfer and play music. For example, you can play and record digital music on your desktop PC or laptop, and the music stays in one format. You can transfer that music to and from your portable digital music player.

Windows Media Player for the Pocket PC allows you to download and record digital music on the Pocket PC. The Pocket PC is small enough to put in your pocket so that you can take your music with you. You can listen to your music by using the internal speaker or a set of headphones attached to the stereo headphone jack.

If you want to play videos in addition to music, you will need to download the latest version of Windows Media Player for Pocket PC from *http://www.microsoft.com/windows/windowsmedia/en/download/default .asp*. The version of Windows Media Player that comes preinstalled on the Pocket PC can play only digital music. After downloading the latest version, you can play some of your favorite movie trailers or even your own home movies on the Pocket PC. This chapter will focus on Media Player version 7, which plays both video and music.

Music Formats and Storage

You can record digital music in various formats. The two most popular formats are MPEG Audio Layer-3 (MP3) and Windows Media (WMA). Files in these formats can be played with both Windows Media Player on the desktop PC and Windows Media Player for the Pocket PC. When you create a digital music file from a CD (also known as *ripping*), you can choose the format you want to use. The quality of the two formats is about the same, but a WMA music file is about half the size of the same song recorded using the MP3 format.

As with any portable electronic computing device, storage is critical. Most Pocket PCs come from the factory with either 16 megabytes (MB) or 32 MB of storage. Music and video files can quickly fill the Pocket PC's internal storage. If you plan to keep several music files or videos on your Pocket PC, you might want to consider other storage options, such as CompactFlash storage cards.

Windows Media Player 7 for the Pocket PC can also handle secure music files protected with Microsoft Windows Media Rights Manager, the Microsoft Digital Rights Management (DRM) technology. The DRM technology is designed to protect intellectual property such as music, movies, and books. Many major record companies and retailers are offering secure music for online purchase. Secure music files have built-in rules that specify how and where that music can be played. No configuration steps are necessary when transferring DRM files. The only thing you need to remember when dealing with DRM files is that you must use Windows Media Player on the desktop PC to transfer files from the desktop PC to the Pocket PC.

Creating MP3 and WMA Music

Before you can play digital music on the Pocket PC, you must create the WMA or MP3 files on the desktop PC. I recommend using Windows

Media Player 7 tools on the desktop PC. However, other tools are available for creating MP3 or WMA files.

Because of the number of components involved in the process—the desktop PC, the audio CD, Pocket PC connectivity through Microsoft ActiveSync, and so on—ripping a CD is somewhat complicated. It does get easier with practice, so hang in there.

First you need to make sure you have the proper components and the right software installed. You need to have a desktop PC or laptop with a CD-ROM player capable of playing audio CDs. You need to install Windows Media Player 7 on the desktop PC. If you have Microsoft Windows Me, this application is already installed. If not, you can obtain it from *http://www.microsoft.com/windows/windowsmedia/en/download/default.asp*. You also must have your Pocket PC configured to connect successfully through ActiveSync. Now you're ready to get an audio file onto the Pocket PC.

Downloading Music to the Pocket PC

You obtain digital music by using the Windows Media Player on the desktop PC to transform songs from an audio CD into digital music in the form of WMA or MP3 files. Once you have these files, follow these steps to transfer the files to the Pocket PC:

1. Use the Windows Media Player interface to locate the files that you want to transfer to your Pocket PC. With Windows Media Player on the desktop PC open, click Portable Device on the left side of the window.

2. You will see two windows. The left window represents the content on the desktop PC. The window on the right represents the content on the Pocket PC. Select the source location of your MP3 or WMA files from the drop-down list at the top of the Music To Copy window.

3. Place a check mark next to the files that you want to copy to your Pocket PC.

4. Be sure that you can see the content of the Pocket PC within
the right window. If you do not see the content, make sure that
your Pocket PC is connected correctly.

5. From the drop-down list in the window on the right, choose to
store the music files either in the Pocket PC or on the storage card.

6. Click Copy Music in the upper left corner of the window. You
will see the word Copying next to the names of files that you
are copying. When the files are finished copying, you will see
the word Complete next to the names of the files. You will also
see the names of the files listed within the Music On Device
window on the right.

Playing Music

After you have downloaded your music to the Pocket PC, you're ready
to play the music. To play MP3 or WMA music files on your Pocket PC,
follow these steps:

1. Tap Start, and then tap Windows Media.

2. Tap Playlist at the bottom of the Windows Media Player screen.

3. Select a song to play from the Playlist menu, and then tap the
Play icon at the bottom of the screen.

> **Note**   If you do not see the song you want to play, tap the
> Playlist drop-down menu at the top of the screen and
> select your song from a different playlist.

Playing Videos

Windows Media Player 7 supports Windows Media Audio/Video (WMV)
files. The desktop PC also uses the WMV format. Before you play a video
file on your Pocket PC, you should download it. To download a video
file, follow the same steps you would follow to download music. Once
you have the video file on your Pocket PC, you can play it by following these steps:

1. Be sure that you have the default skin selected for Windows
   Media Player 7. You can get the default skin by tapping Start
   and then tapping Windows Media 7.

2. Tap Playlist at the bottom of the screen to display the playlist
   screen.

3. From the playlist screen, select the video you want to play, and
   then tap the Play icon at the bottom of the screen.

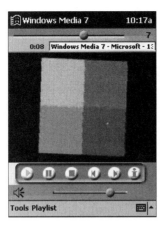

The video will play in the space provided. If the video does not quite fit into the space provided, tap the Tools menu and select Settings. From there you can change the settings of the Oversized Video section to best suit the video area on the screen. You might need to select Crop To Fit or 50% Size for a better-fitting video.

Skins

You might not have heard the term *skins* in reference to digital media before. In the case of Windows Media Player, the skin is a graphic or audio file that customizes the look of the player: the graphical layout of the buttons, the background colors, and the graphics. Windows Media Player 7 for the Pocket PC lets you download skins to your Pocket PC and change them whenever you like. See the section "Changing Skins" later in this chapter for more information on where you can find skins on the Internet.

Creating Custom Playlists

When you press the play button on your CD player, the songs typically play one right after the other, in the order they're listed on the CD. Windows Media Player for the Pocket PC is configured the same way. However, you can also choose which songs to play and in what order you want to play them. You can also customize lists of your own favorite types of music. For example, you can make a playlist that contains only rock music, only classical music, or only jazz. Or you can have a series of playlists organized by artist. The possibilities are limitless. To create a playlist for your favorite songs, follow these steps:

1. Tap Playlist at the bottom of the Windows Media Player 7 window.

2. In the upper left corner of the playlist screen, select All Playlists from the drop-down menu.

3. Tap the New button and give your new playlist a name.

4. Tap OK in the upper right corner. The Add Content screen appears.

5. Place check marks next to the songs that you want to appear in your new playlist. Once you have your songs selected, tap OK in the upper right corner.

6. To hear your playlist, select the playlist from the drop-down menu in the upper left corner of the playlist screen and tap OK in the upper right corner. The first song on the playlist will begin to play.

You can change the order of the songs on the playlist by selecting the song that you want to move and then tapping the up or down arrow at the bottom of the screen to change the order. To delete a song from the playlist, highlight it and tap the X at the bottom of the screen. This will delete the song only from the playlist, not from your Pocket PC. To add a new song to the playlist, tap the green plus sign (+) at the bottom of the screen. The Add Content screen displays all the Windows Media files on your Pocket PC. You can select any song from this list.

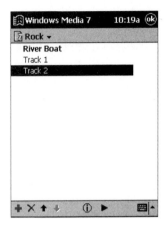

Changing Skins

Several Web sites offer different skins that you can download. You can choose from a wide selection of skins for Windows Media Player for the Pocket PC on the Windows Media Web site at *http://www.microsoft.com/ windows/windowsmedia/en/software/pocket/install.asp*. Download the skins you like to the desktop PC.

> **Note** Before you can change a skin, you must either stop or pause Windows Media Player 7.

Before you install a custom skin to your Pocket PC, you need to follow these steps to make a setting change in ActiveSync:

1. Open ActiveSync on the desktop PC.

2. From the Tools menu, select Options, and then click the Rules tab.

3. Click the Conversion Settings button on the Rules tab to display the File Conversion Properties page.

4. Click the Desktop To Device tab, select BMP Image from the list of file types, and then click the Edit button on this tab.

5. In the Edit Conversion Settings: Bitmap Image dialog box, make sure that *(No conversion)(*.bmp)* is selected in the drop-down list box.

6. Click OK to close the dialog box and the property page.

Now you can install a custom skin. When you download a custom skin from the Windows Media Web site, it comes to the desktop PC as a .zip file. Select Unzip in the Zip Extraction dialog box, and the self-extraction process will start. The file will extract to c:\windows\[*skin name*]. Using the File Explorer feature of ActiveSync, copy the entire skin folder from the desktop PC to the My Pocket PC\Program Files\Windows Media Player 7 folder.

Once you have a custom skin on the Pocket PC, you can change skins by using the Skin Chooser. To change a skin, follow these steps:

1. In Windows Media Player 7, tap the Tools menu at the bottom of the window and select Skin Chooser to display the Skin Chooser screen.

2. Tap the right or left directional button to cycle through the available skins on the Pocket PC.

3. When you find a skin you like, tap OK in the upper right corner of the Skin Chooser screen.

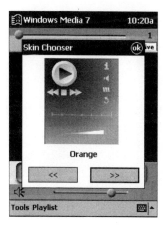

Summing Up

Windows Media Player 7 for the Pocket PC lets you play audio and video files no matter where you are. It also enables you to create playlists of your favorite songs or videos. Different skins let you personalize your player. The Pocket PC really puts the power of multimedia in your pocket.

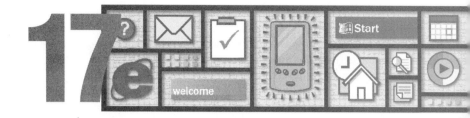

eBooks

Whether you're in a park, on a bus, or in an airplane, you can use the
Pocket PC for work and for play. In addition to playing games and listening to digital music, you can also read electronic books (eBooks)
on the Pocket PC. Microsoft Reader for the Pocket PC is the application that makes this happen. You can download an eBook file from the
Internet to the Pocket PC and then open the file and get lost in a great
eBook.

eBook Formats

Microsoft Reader works with eBooks that are in the .lit format. Whenever
you see a .lit file, you will know that you can read that particular eBook
with Reader. The .lit format is also used on the desktop PC version of
Reader. Any eBook you download for your desktop PC can also be viewed
on the Pocket PC without modification.

An eBook file can range in size from 1 KB to 600 or more KB. A 300-
page book will be approximately a 250-KB eBook. As with digital music, storage space can be a concern. If you don't save your eBooks to a
storage card, be careful not to fill up the main memory of the device by
downloading too many books that you don't plan to read soon. If you
need to have several books on your Pocket PC, use a storage card to
save memory on your device.

One of the best features of Reader is a technology called ClearType, which greatly improves the on-screen text resolution. ClearType smoothes the pixilated edges of the letters, making them look like the text in a printed book.

Like digital music files, eBooks have a few security issues. The Reader application for the Pocket PC also supports the Digital Rights Management (DRM) technology to protect the rights of intellectual property owners. However, there are three different types of DRM security: DRM1, DRM3, and DRM5. The Reader application for the Pocket PC can view books protected with DRM1 and DRM3. It cannot view eBooks protected with DRM5. Unfortunately, DRM5 became a popular format after the Pocket PC was introduced. Most of the locations that offer eBooks will tell you the format the eBook is in. If the eBook is DRM5, it won't function on the Pocket PC. A solution for this problem is in the works, but a release date has not been scheduled.

Finding eBooks

Thousands of eBooks are available online. Some are free, while others can be purchased. Most of the popular online book retailers also sell eBooks. You will find some sample eBooks in the Extras folder on the Microsoft ActiveSync CD that came with your Pocket PC. For more information on where to obtain eBooks, check out *http://www.microsoft.com/reader*.

Downloading an eBook to the Pocket PC

Getting an eBook onto the Pocket PC is simple. To download an eBook from the desktop PC to the Pocket PC, follow these steps:

1. With your Pocket PC connected to the desktop PC, open Active-Sync. From the File menu, select Explore. The Mobile Device window appears. You should now see the contents of the My Documents folder of the Pocket PC.

2. Select an eBook on the desktop PC and drag and drop it into the Mobile Device window. If the file is large, this step might take a few minutes.

> **Note**   You can store eBooks in the main memory or on a storage card. If you choose to keep your eBooks on a storage card, double-click My Pocket PC in the Mobile Device window, open the storage card folder, and then open the My Documents folder on the storage card. You must place eBook files in the My Documents folder in the main memory of the device or in the My Documents folder on the storage card.

3. Once the file copy process is complete, the eBook is ready to be read.

Reading an eBook

To access Reader, tap Start, and then tap Microsoft Reader. The first screen that opens is the Library.

Within the Library, you can see all the books that you have on both the Pocket PC and on the storage card. The Microsoft Reader Guidebook and two fairy tales are eBooks that come preinstalled on most Pocket PCs.

> **Note** If you do not see your newly downloaded eBook in the list, tap the word Library in the lower left corner of the screen to refresh the list of eBooks.

To open an eBook, tap the title or tap the icon next to the title. The cover page of that eBook opens. From there you can open the first page, the table of contents, the most recently read page, or even the furthest-read page. To begin reading, just tap one of these items.

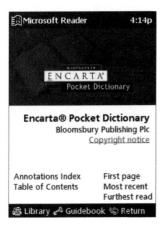

To change pages in an eBook, tap the page direction arrow in the upper right corner of the screen. You can also use the hardware scroll buttons on the side or front of the Pocket PC to change the pages either forward or backward.

To delete a book, go to the Library screen, and then tap and hold the book title. Select Delete from the menu that appears. This will delete the eBook from the Pocket PC only—you will not delete any copies of the eBook that you might have on the desktop PC.

Special Features

Reader has several features that you can use to make reading an eBook an interactive experience. If an eBook dictionary is installed on your Pocket PC, you can use Reader to look up a word in eBook you're reading. You can also use Reader for making annotations and taking notes within the text of the eBook. For example, you might want to make a note or even add a drawing. To access these features, simply tap and hold the word where you want a note, drawing, highlight, or bookmark to appear, and then select the function from the pop-up menu.

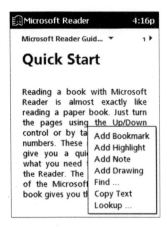

You can also copy text from the eBook and paste it into another document on the Pocket PC, such as a Pocket Word document or e-mail. To copy and paste text, follow these steps:

1. Highlight the text that you want to copy, and then tap and hold it.

2. Select Copy Text from the pop-up menu.

3. Open another document on your Pocket PC, and paste the text in the desired place.

All annotations that have been made to the eBook are recorded in the Annotations Index. You can access the Annotations Index by tapping the title of the eBook and then selecting Annotations Index from the drop-down menu.

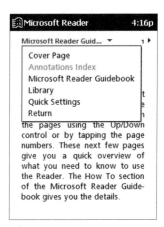

Audio Books

If you have a long commute to work or you do a lot of traveling, you might like to have a book read to you. You can install an application called the Audible Manager to listen to audio books. This application, available from Audible.com, works in conjunction with Reader. Once you've installed Audible Manager, you can download audio books from Audible.com. Audio books will show up in the list of eBooks in the Library. To open the audio book, simply tap it. You will see a cover page with controls at the bottom of the window.

Summing Up

With hundreds of eBooks available, you won't lack for something to read,
even if you're on the road. Microsoft Reader for the Pocket PC uses
ClearType to make eBooks easy to read on your Pocket PC. ClearType
is available only in Microsoft Reader. And with the addition of audio
books from Audible.com, you can even listen to audio books using the
Reader application.

Index

Numbers

16K color, 75

A

Access, Pocket, 30–31
ActiveSync
  AvantGo, 32, 35–37
  Calendar, 25–27
  contacts, 27, 111
  data options, 24–32
  e-mail, 27–29, 94–96
  Ethernet, 64–65
  favorites, 30, 32–33
  files, 31–32, 33–35
  installing, 21–24
  Mobile Favorites, 32–33
  notes, 123–24
  Pocket Access, 30–31
  Tasks, 29, 118
  troubleshooting, 37–39
active tasks, 116
ActiveX Controls, 75
adding
  appointments, 97–98
  components, 13–18
  information, 9–11
  sheets, 141
  Today screen items, 9
addition. *See* calculations
address book. *See* contacts
addresses, IP, 42, 46, 65
adjusting ISP connection settings, 50–51
agenda, Today screen, 8–9
Agenda view, 102–3
aligning
  cell data, 139–40
  screen, 5
all day appointments, 99–100
alphabetically sorting contacts, 106–7
alt DNS servers, 48
America Online e-mail, 88
animated GIFs, 76
annotations, eBook, 163
AOL e-mail, 88

applications overview, 4–5
appointments
  adding to Calendar, 97–98
  all-day, 99–100
  categorizing, 100–101
  changing, 99
  contrasted with tasks, 113
  copying, 104
  moving, 104
  recurring, 99
  removing, 104
  setting reminders, 98–99
  synchronizing, 25–27
  Today screen, 8–9
  views, 102–3
AT&T, 68
attachments
  e-mail, 28, 92, 94, 96, 134–35
  voice recordings to notes, 121
Audible.com, 164
Audible Manager, 164
audio
  books, 164
  recording, 11, 121, 127–28
Authentication, user, 76
Auto-complete URL, 75
Autofit, 140–41
AvantGo, 32, 35–37, 76

B

bar code scanner, 18
baud rate
  ISP connection, 44
  remote synchronization, 57
  wireless connections, 72
Bluetooth, 17
BMP file format, 76
books. *See* audio, books; eBooks
borders, 140
browsing
  Internet, 76–82
  offline, 76, 82–84
burned ROM, 3–4

C

cables, 38, 62
caching, 75
calculations, 144
Calendar
  adding appointments, 97–98
  all-day appointments, 99–100
  categorizing appointments, 100–101
  copying appointments, 104
  moving appointments, 104
  out of office, 99–100
  recurring appointments, 99
  removing appointments, 104
  setting reminders, 98–99
  synchronizing, 25–27
  Today screen, 8–9
  vacations, 99–100
  views, 102–3
call waiting, 52
cards
  CF, 13–18, 69–70
  digital phone, 17, 69
  Ethernet, 62
  PCMCIA, 14, 70
Cascading Style Sheets, 75
categorizing
  appointments, 100–101
  contacts, 108–10
  tasks, 115–16
CDMA, 68
CDPD, 68
cell formats
  changing, 138–40
  editing, 138–40
cell phones, 68–69
cells
  deleting, 142–43
  formatting, 138–40
  inserting, 142–43
Cellular Digital Packet Data. See CDPD
cellular networks, 68
CF cards, 13–18, 69–70
changing
  appointments, 99
  cell formats, 138–40
  contact categories, 109
  eBook pages, 162
Character Recognizer, 10, 120, 127, 138
ClearType, 160

CMOS settings, 39
Code Division Multiple Access. See CDMA
color, 75
columns, 140–41, 145
combining data, 24
CompactFlash, 13–18, 69
complete tasks, 116, 117
components, adding, 13–18
COM port connections, 21
compression settings, 47
configuring
  AvantGo, 36
  e-mail, 88–92
  Pocket PC for Ethernet Sync, 62–64
  wireless connections, 71–74
connections
  initiating, 48–50
  Internet Explorer, 80–81
  ISP, 41–52
  protocols, 42
  types, to desktop, 20–21
  wireless, 17, 67–74
contacts
  categorizing, 108–10
  creating, 105–6
  finding, 106–8
  missing, 110
  removing, 111–12
  sending, 110–11
  sorting, 106–10
  synchronizing, 27, 111
controls, downloading, 76
cookies, 76, 81–82
copying
  appointments, 104
  eBook text, 163
  files, 31, 33–35
  text, 130–31
corporate networks, 49, 55–60, 62, 81
creating
  e-mail, 93
  music files, 150–51
  notes, 119–21
  Pocket Excel documents, 137–38
  Pocket Word documents, 126
  Pocket Word document templates, 128
  tasks, 114–15
credit cards, dialing with, 74
cursor, mouse, 6

customizing
adding components, 13–18
connection settings, 45
Internet browsing, 78–82
music playlists, 154–56
skins, 156–58
Today screen, 9
wireless connection settings, 73–74
cutting text, 130–31

D

data
alignment, 139–40
combining, 24
replacing, 24
Data islands, 76
date, task, 117
Day view, 102–3
default
home page, 79
template, 130
delay, dialing, 52, 74
deleting
appointments, 104
cells, 142–43
contacts, 111–12
eBooks, 162
notes, 123
partnerships, 39
sheets, 141
songs, 155–56
tasks, 117
Today screen items, 9
desktop
synchronizing (see synchronization)
types of connections to, 20–21
DHTML, 76
dialing options, ISP connections, 51–52
dial-up connections, remote
synchronization, 57–59
dictionary, 162–63
digital phone card, 17, 69
disabling call waiting, 52
division. See calculations
DNS servers, 47–48
documents, Pocket Excel. See also
spreadsheets
calculations, 144
creating, 137–38

documents, Pocket Excel, *continued*
deleting cells, 142–43
formatting, 138–41
functions, 144
inserting cells, 142–43
modifying sheets, 141–42
passwords, 146–47
sorting columns, 145
special symbols, 144–45
viewing, 147–48
documents, Pocket Word
audio recording, 127–28
copying text, 130–31
creating, 126
cutting text, 130–31
drawing mode, 132–33
e-mail, 134–35
file types, 130
formatting, 133–34
input methods, 127–28
opening, 126
pasting text, 130–31
recording mode, 132–33
saving, 129
sending, 135
storage, 130
templates, 128, 130
typing mode, 132–33
writing mode, 132–33
domain, 49
Domain Name System servers. See DNS
servers
downloading
controls, 76
eBooks, 160–61
file attachments, 96
fonts, 76
music, 151–52
videos, 153
drag-and-drop, files, 34
drawing mode, 132–33
drivers, Ethernet, 64
DRM, 150, 160

E

eBooks
annotations, 163
audio, 164
changing pages, 162

Index

eBooks, *continued*
   ClearType, 160
   copying text, 163
   deleting, 162
   dictionary, 162–63
   downloading, 160–61
   finding online, 160
   formats, 159–60
   Library, 161–62
   opening, 162
   reading, 161–62
   security, 160
   storage, 159, 161
ECMA-262, 76
e-mail
   attachments, 28, 92, 94, 96, 134–35
   configuring, 88–92
   creating, 93
   documents, 134–35
   offline mode, 95
   receiving, 92–93
   sending, 28, 92–93
   sending links, 78
   synchronizing, 27–29, 94–96
   types, 87–88
   voice recording, 11
entering information, 9–11
Ethernet, remote synchronization, 61–65
Excel. *See* Pocket Excel
expanding Pocket PC, 13–18

F

favorites
   Internet, 82–84
   Internet Explorer, 76
   synchronizing, 30, 32–33
file attachments, 28, 92, 94, 96, 134–35
file format, converting, 34
files
   copying, 31, 33–35
   documents, 130
   eBook format, 159–60
   formats, 76
   moving, 12
   storage, 150
   synchronizing, 31–32, 33–35
   temporary Internet, 80
finding contacts, 106–8
finding eBooks, 160

flashable ROM, 4
floating frames, 76
fonts, 76, 133–34, 140
formats
   eBook, 159–60
   e-mail, 87–88
   file, 34, 76
   music, 150
formatting
   cells, 138–40
   columns, 140–41
   Pocket Excel documents, 138–41
   Pocket Word documents, 133–34
   rows, 140–41
frames, floating, 76
freezing panes, 147
functions, 144

G

GIF file format, 76
global positioning system, 16
Global Systems for Mobile
   Communications. *See* GSM
GPS, 16
GSM, 68

H

handwriting, 10, 133
hardware
   overview, 2–4
   wireless, 68–71
header compression settings, 47
hiding rows and columns, 140
history, Internet Explorer, 80
home networks, remote
   synchronization, 55–60
home page, default, 79
HTML, 76

I

icons
   keyboard, 9
   paper clip, 94
   pencil, 120
IMAP4, 87, 88–92
Inbox, synchronizing, 27–29, 94–96
Index, Annotations, 163–64
information, entering, 9–11

infrared
  connections, 20–21
  ports, 68–69
  sending Pocket Word documents, 135
initiating connections, 48–50
input methods, Pocket Word
  documents, 127–28
inserting
  cells, 142–43
  symbols, 144–45
installing ActiveSync, 21–24
Internet. *See also* Web
  browsing, 76–82
  favorites, 82–84
  ISP connection, 41–52
  proxy servers, 77, 81
  sending links, 78
  temporary files, 80
Internet Explorer
  connections, 80–81
  customizing, 78–82
  default home page, 79
  favorites, 82–84
  history, 80
  supported technologies, 75–76
  synchronizing Mobile Favorites, 32–33
  views, 77–78
Internet Message Access Protocol version
  4. *See* IMAP4
Internet Service Provider (ISP) connections
  adjusting settings, 50–51
  advanced settings, 46–48
  creating, 43
  dialing options, 51–52
  ending, 51
  initiating, 48–50
  overview, 41–43
  wireless, 72–74
inventory control, 18
IP addresses, 42, 46, 65
ISP e-mail types, 87

J

Java, 76
JPEG file format, 76
Jscript 3.0, 76

K

keyboard, 9, 120, 127, 138

L

LANs, 61
laptops, infrared connections to, 20–21
Library, 161–62
links
  highlighting, 76
  radio, 17
  sending, 78
lit format, 159–60
local area networks. *See* LANs
locating specific contacts, 106–108

M

mail. *See* e-mail
mapping, 16
math. *See* calculations
Media Player. *See* Windows Media Player
meetings. *See* appointments
memory. *See also* storage
  CF cards, 15
  ROM, 3–4
memo templates, 128
menus
  shortcut, 6
  Start, 6–9
messages. *See* e-mail
Microsoft Digital Rights Management. *See*
  DRM
Microsoft Windows Media Rights
  Manager, 150
Mobile Favorites, 32–33, 82–84
mobile phones, 17
modems
  adding, 15–16
  ISP connection, 42–43, 44
  remote synchronization, 55–60
  wireless, 70
modes, Pocket Word, 132–33
Month view, 102–3
mouse, 6
moving
  appointments, 104
  files, 34
  notes, 122–23
Mozilla 2.0, 76
MP3, 150–51
MPEG Audio Layer-3. *See* MP3
multiplication. *See* calculations

music
  creating files, 150–51
  custom playlists, 154–56
  deleting songs, 155–56
  downloading, 151–52
  file storage, 150
  formats, 150
  playing, 152–53

N
name entry sort, contacts, 107–8
navigating, 6–9
networks
  cellular, 68
  corporate, 49, 55–60, 62, 81
  LAN, 61
Nextcell, Inc., 70
notes
  creating, 119–21
  deleting, 123
  moving, 122–23
  option, 31
  removing, 123
  renaming, 122–23
  sorting, 122–23
  synchronizing, 123–24
  voice recordings, 121
number format, 139

O
offline
  browsing, 76, 82–84
  e-mail, 95
online eBooks, 160
on/off switch, 5
on-screen keyboard, 9
opening
  eBooks, 162
  Pocket Word documents, 126
operating system, 3, 4
organizing appointments, 100–101
Outbox, synchronizing, 28–29
out of office, 99–100

P
pages, eBooks, 162
panes, viewing, 147
paper clip icon, 94
partnerships, 39

partnerships, deleting, 162
passwords, 49, 81–82, 146–47
pasting text, 130–31, 163
PCMCIA cards, 14, 70
pencil icon, 120
penmanship, 10, 133
peripheral devices, CompactFlash, 13–18
phone card, 17, 69
phones, cell, 68–69
PIM, defined, 1
playing
  music, 152–53, 154–56
  videos, 153–54
playlists, 154–56
Pocket Access, 30–31
Pocket Excel
  creating documents, 137–38
  deleting cells, 142–43
  formatting documents, 138–41
  functions, 144
  inserting cells, 142–43
  modifying sheets, 141–42
  passwords, 146–47
  sorting columns, 145
  special symbols, 144–45
  viewing, 147–48
Pocket PC
  adding components, 13–18
  features, 2–5
  hardware overview, 2–4
  software overview, 4–5
  types of connections to desktop, 20–21
Pocket Spider, 70
Pocket Word
  document templates, 128, 130
  document text, 130–31
  e-mail, 134–35
  formatting documents, 133–34
  input methods, 127–28
  modes, 132–33
  new documents, 126
  opening documents, 126
  saving documents, 129
  sending documents, 135
  settings, 129–30
  types of document files, 130
Point-to-Point Protocol. See PPP
POP3, 87, 88–92
portable keyboard, 127

Index

Spider, Pocket, 70
splitting panes, 147
spreadsheets. *See also* documents, Pocket
  Excel
  calculations, 144
  deleting cells, 142–43
  functions, 144
  inserting cells, 142–43
  sorting columns, 145
  special symbols, 144–45
Sprint, 68
Start menu, 6–9
status, task, 117
storage. *See also* memory
  eBooks, 159, 161
  music files, 150
  Pocket Word documents, 130
Style Sheets, Cascading, 75
subject, task, 117
subscriptions, 76
subtraction. *See* calculations
symbols, inserting, 144–45
symbols, special, 144–45
synchronization
  AvantGo, 32, 35–37
  Calendar, 25–27
  connections, 20–21
  contacts, 27, 111
  data options, 24–32
  e-mail, 27–29, 94–96
  favorites, 30, 32–33, 82–84
  files, 31–32, 33–35
  Inbox, 27–29, 94–96
  installing ActiveSync, 21–24
  Mobile Favorites, 32–33
  notes, 123–24
  remote, Ethernet, 61–65
  remote, modem, 55–60
  settings, 25
  Tasks, 29, 118
  troubleshooting, 37–39

T

tap and hold, 5–6
tasks
  categorizing, 115–16
  completed, 117
  contrasted with appointments, 113
  creating, 114–15
  deleting, 117

tasks, *continued*
  sorting, 117
  synchronizing, 29, 118
TCP/IP, 42
template, default, 130
templates, Pocket Word documents,
  128, 130
temporary Internet files, 80
text
  copying, 130–31
  copying eBook, 163
  Pocket Word documents, 130–31,
    133–34
  wrapping cell, 140
time zone, 5
Today screen, 8–9
Transcriber, 10, 120, 127, 138
Transfer Control Protocol/Internet
  Protocol. *See* TCP/IP
troubleshooting
  DNS server, 48
  modems, 59–60
  remote synchronization, Ethernet, 65
  remote synchronization, modem, 59–60
  synchronization, 37–39
TXT file format, 76
types
  CF cards, 15–16
  CF card slots, 14–16
  document files, 130
  e-mail, 87–88
typing mode, 132–33

U

UA string, 76
unfreezing panes, 147
unhiding rows and columns, 140
unresolved items, 39
upgrading, 4
URL, Auto-complete, 75
USB connections, 20
User Agent string, 76
User Authentication, 76
usernames, 49, 81–82
utilities, handwriting recognition, 10

V

vacations, 99–100
VBscript, 76

Verizon, 68
videos
file storage, 150
playing, 153–54
viewing
contact categories, 109
Pocket Excel documents, 147–48
sheets, 142
views
Calendar, 102–3
Internet Explorer, 77–78
Virtual Reality Modeling Language. *See*
VRML
voice recording, 11, 121, 127–28
VoiceStream, 68
VRML, 76

W

WAV file format, 76
Web. *See also* Internet
AvantGo, 32, 35–37
browsing, 76–82
e-mail, 88
favorites, 82–84
Mobile Favorites, 32–33
proxy servers, 77, 81
sending links, 78
Week view, 102–3
Welcome Wizard, 5
Windows 98, remote synchronization, 59
Windows 2000, remote
synchronization, 59
Windows Internet Names Service servers.
See WINS servers
Windows Media. *See* WMA
Windows Media Player
creating files, 150–51
downloading music, 151–52
file storage, 150
music formats, 150
playing music, 152–53, 154–56
playing videos, 153–54
skins, 154, 156–57
WINS servers, 47–48
wireless connections
advantages, 67
cell phones, 68–69
configuring, 71–74
hardware, 68–71
ISP connections, 72–74

wireless connections, *continued*
Pocket PC features, 17
technologies, 68
wizards
installing ActiveSync, 21–24
Welcome, 5
WMA, 150–51
WMV, 153–54
Word. *See* Pocket Word
worksheets. *See* documents, Pocket Excel;
spreadsheets
World Wide Web. *See* Web
wrapping cell text, 140
writing by hand, 10, 133
writing mode, 132–33
WWW. *See* Web

XYZ

XBM file format, 76
XML, 76
Year view, 102–3
zooming, 147–48

Steve Seroshek

Steve Seroshek has been involved with Windows CE–related products since 1995 and has become a well-known figure in the Windows CE space. As a Microsoft Support Professional for Windows CE products for the past three years, Steve has written and presented numerous technical articles about the palm-size PC, handheld PC, and Pocket PC. Steve is currently a product manager in the Mobility Division at Microsoft, where he is responsible for the PocketPC.com Web site and other mobility-related Web sites.

A graduate of Washington State University with a B.S. in electrical engineering, Steve is also a Microsoft Certified Systems Engineer and a part-time instructor of Microsoft operating systems at a local technical college. Originally from Centralia, Washington, Steve now lives in Auburn, Washington, with his wife, Karolyn, and his two dogs and two cats.

The manuscript for this book was prepared and galleyed using Microsoft Word 98. Pages were composed by Microsoft Press using Adobe PageMaker 6.52 for Windows, with text in Garamond and display type in Helvetica Condensed. Composed pages were delivered to the printer as electronic prepress files.

Cover Designer: Patrick Lanfear
Interior Graphic Designer: James D. Kramer
Principal Compositor: Gina Cassill
Interior Artist: Joel Panchot
Principal Copy Editor: Shawn Peck
Indexer: Patti Schiendelman

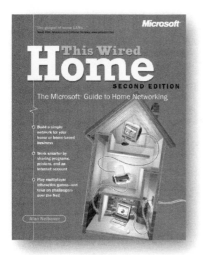

Get a **Free**
*e-mail newsletter, updates,
special offers, links to related books,
and more when you*
register on line!

Register your Microsoft Press® title on our Web site and you'll get
a FREE subscription to our e-mail newsletter, *Microsoft Press Book
Connections.* You'll find out about newly released and upcoming books
and learning tools, online events, software downloads, special offers and
coupons for Microsoft Press customers, and information about major
Microsoft® product releases. You can also read useful additional information about all the titles we publish, such as detailed book descriptions,
tables of contents and indexes, sample chapters, links to related books
and book series, author biographies, and reviews by other customers.

Registration is easy. Just visit this Web page and fill in your information:

http://www.microsoft.com/mspress/register

Microsoft®

Proof of Purchase

The Pocket PC
0-7356-1159-9

CUSTOMER NAME

Microsoft Press, PO Box 97017, Redmond, WA 98073-9830